50

D0230120

THESE ARE THE GERMAN THRUSTS

QUEUES FORM TO JOIN NEW DEFENCE CORPS

Ready to shoot parachute troops

Daily Express Staff Reporter

MR. EDEN, the new War Secretary, asked the country last night for Local Defence Volunteers who, in uniform and with arms, but without pay, will help to protect us from the menace of para-troops.

And almost as soon as he had finished broadcasting the volunteers rolled up, and thousands had been registered.

These stalwarts will be, in the main, boys of the old brigade. Mr. Eden said enlistment would cover the ages 17 to 65, but middle-aged men will form the body of the corps.

They will be enrolled for the duration, but will not be required to live away from home. Applicants must be reasonably fit and have a knowledge of firearms.

TOO QUICK !

Mr. Eden asked volunteers to enter their names at the local police station. They acted so quickly that in some districts they arrived before the police knew anything about the invitation. Many telephoned.

Scotland-yard was asked for instructions. They were told to take names and addresses: special constables helped. People were still coming in at midnight.

An ex-soldier of Surbiton told me that, although he hurried to the station as soon as the broadcast was finished, there was already a queue waiting. More

are plenty of hose ardour is h formidable, ing—including e hard earned

SURRENDER OF THESE CITIES PRECEDED 'CEASE FIRE' ORDER

EMDEN

HOLLAND

Groningen

AMSTERDAM

Zwolle

Schiphol

UTRECHT

ARNHEM

ROTTERDAM

DORDRECHT

Moerdyk

Grave

R. Rhine

FLUSHING

Venlo

OSTEND · Bruges

Ghent

ANTWERP

BELGIUM

LOUVAIN

BRUSSELS

Tirlemont

AACHEN

LILLE · Roubaix

NAMUR

LIEGE

R. Ourthe

·Arras

Charleroi

ARDENNES

R. Rhine

R. Moselle

Cambrai

Dinant

SEDAN

Arlon

R. Saar

R. Somme

River Meuse

Sierck

Thionville

SAARBRUCKEN

FRANCE

MAGINOT LINE

WISSEMBURG

KARLS-RHUE

GERMANY LAUNCHES GENERAL ATTACK ON 450 MILE FRONT *into 4 countries*

Drawn by Rip Files

0 20 40 60 MILES

▶ BACK PAGE, COLUMN THREE

Dad's Army

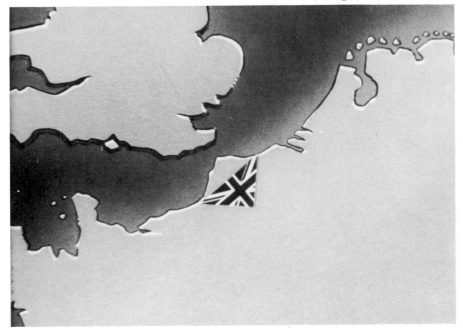

DAD'S ARMY

by Jimmy Perry and David Croft

ELM TREE BOOKS/HAMISH HAMILTON
LONDON

The publishers acknowledge with thanks the
co-operation of the BBC

First published in Great Britain 1975
by Elm Tree Books Ltd
90 Great Russell Street, London WC1

SBN 241 89251 1

Designed by Lawrence Edwards

Photographs supplied by
BBC Enterprises, BBC Publicity
Radio Times, Imperial War Museum
Punch, and Historical Newspaper Services

Photoset and printed in Great Britain by
REDWOOD BURN LIMITED Trowbridge & Esher

Contents

Foreword

IN THE LAST decade we have seen television spread its influence into the older media of entertainment. Firstly, by turning successful series into films, then into radio series and latterly invading the theatre itself. The latest fashionable venture is the long playing record and the publication of scripts.

It is fitting, therefore, that *Dad's Army* should have a place on the bandwagon. In fact, it is entitled to a special place, for it has become a legend in its time. Perhaps no television series has had quite such a universal appeal in the history of electronic entertainment. It has crossed the barriers of age, creed, and a multiplicity of races. No one can put a finger on any particular reason for such phenomenal success—it is a chemistry which has worked almost without the conscious knowledge of the participants.

There is, however, one root ingredient without which nothing could have worked, and that is the writing of the scripts. There have been many talented scriptwriters, but Jimmy Perry and David Croft have achieved a miracle of near perfection in situation building, character drawing, authenticity, and a mixture of slapstick and subtle comedy which is not only acceptable to their vastly divergent audiences, but to their actors at the FIRST READING! This is what makes their work unique in my experience. Rarely in my years of work in long-running television series has a script been acceptable to all the actors at first sight, and anyone who has known the misery of spending days of precious rehearsal time in re-writing scripts will know what I am talking about.

The fact, then, that the scripts you are about to read hardly differ by a word from the ones we first read is, in my opinion, the most important single contributory factor to the success of the show.

I hope you enjoy reading them as much as we enjoyed performing them.

How Dad's Army began

8   DURING THE SUMMER of 1967, I was walking through St James's Park and in the distance I could hear the bands playing for the changing of the guard. The red tunics of the soldiers made a brave sight—what a difference from the drab khaki battledress of the war years, when the Home Guard had a spell of duty at the Palace. I thought back to the time when, as a boy, I had been a member of the Home Guard at Watford. Who remembered the Home Guard now? Nobody. I walked quickly to the Westminster Public Library and looked through the shelves; not a single book on it. I asked a young library assistant if she could help me. 'Never heard of it,' she said.

That evening I was sitting on the train on my way out to Stratford, where I was working with Joan Littlewood's company as an actor, when it suddenly hit me! The Home Guard—what an idea for a television comedy series. I quickly made a few notes, and the next morning started on the first script. In three days it was finished. The question was what to do next. I realised that I could not possibly tackle a series like this on my own. I needed someone to work with, but who? A few weeks later fate intervened in the person of David Croft. I was playing a part in a comedy series which he was producing at the BBC, and I gave him the script to read. His reaction was instantaneous. 'What a terrific idea!' said David. 'Then what about writing it with me?' said I. We shook hands and it was the start of a great partnership.

The rest is history. Within two weeks the BBC had commissioned the show, and since then David and I have written over seventy episodes together. So many people have helped to make the series a success, but I would like to pay a special tribute to Huw Wheldon, Bill Cotton, Michael Mills and the late Tom Sloane, who had so much faith in it right from the start, and one extra thank you to Michael Mills, who gave it the title *Dad's Army*.

JIMMY PERRY

left David Croft
right Jimmy Perry

IT IS ONLY a little place. People with not too much money can retire there to spend their declining years in small houses and bungalows. In happier times, a string of neat comfortable Georgian guest houses could accommodate well-mannered families during the summer months. Mother and father could listen to the band while the children played on the fine clean sand, or the whole family could watch the Pierrots. Hopeful fishermen dangled their lines from the Pier. Stone's Amusement Arcade housed some slot machines where for a penny you could watch a fireman slide up a ladder to rescue a woman from a burning house or see a murderer hanged or a French aristocrat guillotined.

The Novelty Rock Emporium turned out crisp mint rock and giant humbugs. But all that is gone now. The Pier has a twenty-foot gap in the middle, the beach bristles with barbed wire, criss-crossed scaffolding, pill boxes and concrete anti-tank blocks. Stead and Simpsons and Timothy Whites still carry on—so do Jones the Butcher, Frazer the Undertaker, Hodges the Greengrocer and the Marigold Tea Rooms and Mr Mainwaring's Bank.

But the threat across the channel is never far from their thoughts. Hitler is there with all his military might and make no mistake about it, when he launches his attack against Britain, Walmington-on-Sea will be in the front line.

Asleep in the Deep

Mainwaring, Wilson and Pike are looking out through a slit in a command post made of sandbags and planks. In the background are the other members of the platoon. They are all wearing steel helmets and equipment. We can hear the drone of planes and ack ack fire. Pike is sucking his thumb.

MAINWARING   Do take your thumb out of your mouth, boy. You know, Wilson, I'd give everything I possess to have a go at the enemy. I feel so helpless—our lads are out there, bowling Jerry for six, and here we are, stuck in the pavilion.
Jones and Frazer enter, followed by Private Sponge and two other privates. They all have their bayonets fixed. There is loud ack ack fire.
JONES   Number two patrol reporting, sir.
MAINWARING   Yes, Jones.
JONES   All quiet, sir.
Several loud bangs.
MAINWARING   What?
JONES   I said it's all quiet, sir. When I say 'all quiet', I'm not referring to the noise, if you understand me, sir. The 'all quiet' is official military procedure.

FRAZER   Ach! What the old fool is trying to tell you, Captain Mainwaring, is that we didn't spot any Nazi parachutists.
Frazer starts to unfix his bayonet.
MAINWARING   Why have they got their bayonets fixed, Jones?
JONES   In case the parachutists come floating down, sir. You've got to be ready for the old upward thrust.
Jones thrusts his bayonet upwards. It goes into one of the sandbags and a shower of sand falls on Mainwaring.
JONES   Sorry sir, sorry sir.
He brushes Mainwaring off.
MAINWARING   Pike, bung up that hole. Go and have a rest in the corner, Jones.
JONES   Yes sir, yes sir. Number two patrol at the double—go and have a rest in the corner.
WILSON   I think it's the best place for him.
MAINWARING   (*to Wilson*)   You may well scoff—I like the man's spirit, Wilson. You can see the light of battle in his eye; it's exhilarating.
WILSON   Yes, sir. Awfully good, but rather sandy.
MAINWARING   I wouldn't mind seeing a light of battle in your eyes, that is if you could keep them open long enough. What's the matter, didn't you get any sleep last night?
WILSON   Well you must admit, sir, we've been going at it pretty hard lately. Working at the bank all day, and then being on duty most of the night.
MAINWARING   I'm just as tired as you are, Wilson. But I'm not standing here with a dozey look on my face. As an officer I have to set an example to my men—and you should do the same. Now brighten up.
Pike takes a dirty sweet bag out of his pocket.
PIKE (*to Wilson*)   Uncle Arthur?
WILSON   What?
PIKE   Would you like some hundreds and thousands?
WILSON   Oh, how nice.
Wilson holds out his hand and Pike tips some into his palm.
PIKE   Would you like some, Captain Mainwaring?
MAINWARING   Certainly not!
PIKE   I always have my sweet ration in hundreds and thousands. They weigh light and you get a lot more for your coupons.
MAINWARING   Number three section, get ready for patrol.
Frazer moves down to Mainwaring.
FRAZER   If you ask my opinion, Captain Mainwaring, I think it would be sheer folly for them to go out—sheer folly. That shrapnel is coming down like hail.
MAINWARING   What do you suggest then? That we crouch in this funk hole for the rest of the night?
FRAZER   No, but we can't do very much. We should stay where we are, it's common sense.
MAINWARING   War has got nothing to do with common sense, Frazer. I don't want to skulk in here, I want to get out there and get to grips with the enemy.
WILSON   Don't you think that they're rather high up for that, sir?
Mainwaring glares at him.
JONES   Oh, Captain Mainwaring, that's the sort of talk I like to hear. You know you remind me of a major we had in the trenches in 1916.

He was just like you. Major Willerby D'Arcy his name was, he wasn't a skulking man, didn't do a lot of skulking at all, just couldn't abide crouching and skulking. You should have seen him, sir, top boots polished like glass, monocle glistening in his eye. Wonderful man. Anyhow, one day we was crouching in the bottom of the trench, and he said to us, 'Boys, I've had enough of this. I'm going to get up on that parapet and walk about, just to show those damned Jerries that we're not afraid.' Well he climbed up to the top of the parapet. . .

MAINWARING   I know what you're going to say, Jones—he walked about and didn't get a scratch.

JONES   No, sir, he got shot. In a rather inconvenient place it was; he had to do a lot of crouching after that.

There is a pause. Pike offers the bag to Jones.

PIKE   Would you like a hundred and thousand, Mr Jones?

JONES   Thank you, Pikey.

He holds out his hand. There is a loud explosion, he knocks the bag and the sweets spill on the floor.

PIKE   Oh no. That was a whole week's sweet ration.

Hodges the Warden rushes in.

HODGES   Blimey, that was close. I think it came down in the woods. What are you all hiding in here for? Shouldn't you be out looking for parachutists?

WILSON   Just clear off, will you?

MAINWARING   Yes, mind your own business.

HODGES   Now, don't you start, Napoleon.

JONES   Why aren't you out A. R. Peeing?

HODGES   If you must know, I've been A. R. Peeing all night. I've done my job, mate. All my people are on duty. That's the second bomb we've had tonight, you know.

FRAZER   Where did the first one come down?

HODGES   Only a small one on the pumping station. It's all right, there's no one in it.

MAINWARING   What are you talking about? Godfrey and Walker are on duty there.

HODGES   No one told me.

MAINWARING   We must get down there at once. Wilson, Jones, Frazer, Pike, come with me. Sponge—you take charge here.

HODGES   You can't go interfering. This is an A.R.P. matter.

MAINWARING   Mind your own business.

Pike is bending down.

MAINWARING   What are you doing on the floor, Pike?

PIKE   I'm trying to pick up my hundreds and thousands.

MAINWARING   Come on, you stupid boy.

At the pumping station: on the far wall of the room are about twenty pipes with stopcocks on them. On the other wall is a small grille. Next to it is a manhole cover with bolts on the outside. It is big enough for a man to get through. On a rack are several large spanners. There are two doors. One of them opens and Hodges, Mainwaring, Wilson, Jones, Frazer and Pike rush in.

HODGES   I told you so—there's nobody here.

MAINWARING   They're in the next room. (*He runs over to the other door and pulls it open. A pile of bricks and rubble falls into the room. The passage outside is blocked.*) The wall's collapsed!

Walker's face appears at the grille.

WALKER   Mr Mainwaring! Mr Mainwaring!

JONES   Mr Mainwaring, let me give you a bunk up.

Mainwaring climbs onto a chair to reach the grille.

MAINWARING   Are you all right, Walker?

WALKER   Yes, but I can't get out.

MAINWARING   What's happened?

WALKER   The wall's collapsed against the door. It won't open.

MAINWARING   Where's Godfrey?

WALKER   He's asleep on the bunk.

FRAZER   Did you hear that? Godfrey's asleep! The old fool's asleep on duty, in wartime on active service—that's an offence punishable by death. Did you hear what I said, Mr Mainwaring? Death! Death!

MAINWARING   Oh, do be quiet, Frazer. Why are you both in there, Walker? One of you should have been on duty on the roof.

WALKER   I did my two hours on duty. Then I came down here for Godfrey to relieve me and I couldn't wake him up. It was then that the bomb came down.

MAINWARING   Take Godfrey's name, Wilson.

WILSON   I know his name.

MAINWARING   Write it down. I shall see him in my office tomorrow.

WALKER   You don't understand, Mr Mainwaring. I think he's ill.

MAINWARING   Why?

WALKER   I still can't wake him up. I've tried everything.

MAINWARING   Right. We'll soon get you out of there. Come on, Wilson!

JONES   I'll give you a bunk down.

Mainwaring climbs on the rubble and out into the passage, which is in darkness. Wilson follows.

MAINWARING   It doesn't look too bad. I don't think it will take us long to shift this lot.

HODGES   Wait a minute. You're not doing any shifting, this is an A.R.P. job. Heavy rescue, and I'm taking charge. I'm Chief Warden.

MAINWARING   Rubbish. You're doing nothing of the sort. I'm taking charge.

HODGES   I tell you I'm taking charge.

Wilson has climbed right out into the passage. He flicks his cigarette lighter.

MAINWARING   Those are my men trapped in there, so I'm taking charge and that's that.

WILSON (*holding up his lighter*) Good heavens, look at that, sir.

MAINWARING What?

He climbs up.

WILSON Those huge cracks in the wall.

MAINWARING (*looking right up*) The whole lot could come down any minute.

HODGES (*looking up*) Blimey! Perhaps you're right. Captain Mainwaring, you should be in charge. As you say, they *are* your men.

He moves back.

MAINWARING Keep perfectly still, Wilson. Now hold my hand.

WILSON I beg your pardon?

MAINWARING Hold my hand and we'll creep back into the room.

Everything goes quiet; no one speaks. Mainwaring takes Wilson's hand and they creep gingerly back into the room. They all gather in a tight group round Mainwaring.

MAINWARING (*whispering*) Now, listen to me very carefully, men. Only part of the wall has collapsed. God knows what's holding the rest up. The slightest noise or movement could bring the whole lot down. And we can't wait—Godfrey may be very ill.

FRAZER The question is, how are we going to shift that rubble without bringing the whole wall down on top of us?

MAINWARING There's only one thing for it, men: we must form a chain and pass the rubble back here into this room. I'm afraid it's not going to be too pleasant for whoever's at the head of the chain.

HODGES Pleasant? It's going to be damn dangerous.

JONES Permission to whisper, sir. I should like to volunteer to be the head of the daisy chain. Let me do it sir, let me lead the daisy chain.

MAINWARING No, Jones, we're going to draw lots. (*He takes a diary out of his pocket and tears out the pages*) Now, I shall mark two of these pieces of paper with a cross. Whoever draws them goes to the head of the chain.

He moves away to mark them.

PIKE (*whispering*) Uncle Arthur!

WILSON What is it, Frank?

PIKE I saw them do this in the film *Each Dawn I Die.*

WILSON Really. Who drew the paper with the cross on it?

PIKE The sergeant.

WILSON (*turning on him*) I do wish you wouldn't keep talking about films all the time, Frank. It's so boring.

PIKE Why have you gone all cross, Uncle Arthur?

WILSON I'm not cross. I'm just, er . . . slightly frightened, that's all.

Mainwaring comes back with the pieces of paper screwed up in his hat.

MAINWARING Now there are six pieces of paper screwed up in this hat. . .

HODGES What are you talking about—six pieces? There are only five of you.

MAINWARING I know, but you make six.

HODGES Now wait a minute. This has got nothing to do with me.

FRAZER Ach! I thought so, you're yellow.

JONES You're right there, Jock. He's got a stripe down his back a foot wide.

MAINWARING Quiet. (*Slowly to Hodges*) Now, are you going to take one or not?

There is a long silence. They all stare at Hodges, who looks round at the group and licks his lips.

HODGES   All right, I'll take one. I'm not going to give you lot a chance to have anything on me.
MAINWARING   You first, Wilson.
He offers the hat.
WILSON (*takes a paper and unrolls it*)   Blank.
MAINWARING   Jones.
JONES   Nothing on it, sir.
MAINWARING   Frazer.
Frazer reaches out. Hodges knocks his hand.
HODGES   I'm next. (*He grabs a paper*) Blimey, I've got it.
FRAZER   What a pity. I was going to take that one.
Hodges gives him a terrible glare.
MAINWARING   Right, I'm next. (*He takes a paper and unrolls it. It is blank*) I've got the second one.
JONES   Let me go in your place, sir. You're too young to die. Let me go, let me go.
MAINWARING   No, Jones. I want you to stay in here at the end of the chain. Right, men, take your equipment off, but keep your steel helmets on. (*To Hodges*) Come on, Chief Warden.
They climb through the door into the passage. In the passage the rubble is about three feet high. It is blocking the door into the second room which opens outwards into the passage. Mainwaring and Hodges reach the door. Mainwaring picks up a piece of rubble and hands it to Hodges.
MAINWARING (*whispering to Hodges*)   The slightest sound could bring this wall down. Tell them not to make any noise. Pass it on.
Back in the first room Wilson is standing just outside the door. Frazer is in the doorway with Pike next to him and then Jones. They are passing pieces of rubble along the chain. Jones puts the pieces on the floor. They are moving like a well-oiled machine.
WILSON (*whispering to Frazer*)   Don't make any noise. Pass it on.
FRAZER (*whispering to Pike*)   Don't make any noise, whatever you do. Pass it on.
PIKE (*whispering to Jones*)   Don't make any noise.
JONES   Don't make. . .
Pike hands another bit of rubble to Jones, who puts it on the floor.
WALKER (*shouting through the grille*)   Hey Jonesey, what's going on?
Jones turns to the grille.
JONES   Shut up, Joe, you mustn't make any. . .
Pike passes a brick to Jones, whose hands are not there. The brick drops on his foot. Jones goes purple trying to stifle a shout.

In the corner of the second room is a two-tier bunk. Godfrey is asleep on top of it. At the head of the bunk is a manhole cover with bolts. This is hidden from view by pillows. Further along the wall is a rack with spanners on it. Next to that is the manhole cover leading to the first room. Next is the grille, and beneath that is a tin bath on which Walker had stood to look through the grille. Walker is leaning over the bunk trying to wake Godfrey up.

WALKER   Oh blimey. What's the matter with him? (*He shakes him*) Wake up, Charlie. (*Godfrey has a lovely smile on his face*) He can't be ill. He wouldn't be smiling like that if he was. I wonder if his heart's all right. (*He unbuttons Godfrey's blouse and puts his ear to his chest*) I can't hear anything. (*He unbuttons a woolen waistcoat and listens again*) His heart's not beating. (*He unbuttons Godfrey's shirt and pulls out a*

large piece of thermogene wool) No wonder I can't hear anything. (*He listens again*) That's better. Sound as a bell. (*He crosses to the grille and stands on the tin bath*) Hey Jonesey, what's happening?
Jones's face appears at the grille.
JONES   Don't worry, Joe, we're nearly through. How's Mr Godfrey?
WALKER   I can't make it out. He's sleeping like a baby.
The door opens a few inches and Mainwaring whispers through the crack.
MAINWARING   Walker.
Walker rushes over to the door.

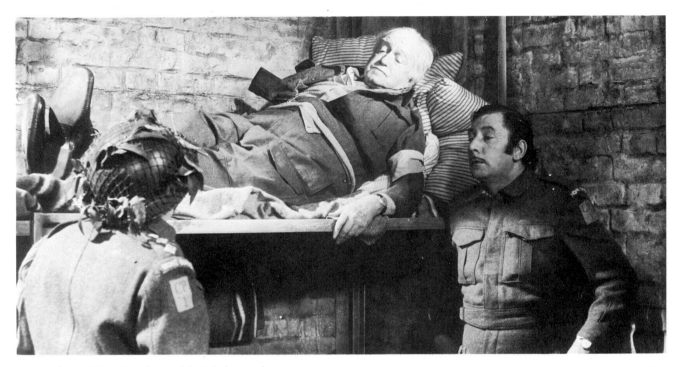

WALKER   Yes, I'm here, Mr Mainwaring.
MAINWARING   Now listen. Push the door from your side very slowly.
Walker pushes the door. It slowly opens about two feet. Mainwaring, Hodges and Wilson squeeze through.
MAINWARING   A bit more. How's Godfrey?
WALKER   I dunno. He looks O.K. Just won't wake up.
Mainwaring crosses to the bunk.
MAINWARING   Godfrey, can you hear me? (*He feels his pulse*) He seems all right.
Frazer and Pike push through the door.
MAINWARING   I thought I told you two to stay in the other room.
FRAZER   Well, if the silly old . . . I mean the poor old man's ill, I want to help.
PIKE   Don't forget I've got my scout badge for first aid, Mr Mainwaring.
MAINWARING   Frazer.
FRAZER   Sir.
MAINWARING   Close the door quietly. And Wilson, tell Jones to stay where he is. And close his door.
WILSON (*speaking through the grille*)   Jonesey, Mr Mainwaring says stay where you are and close the door.
JONES   Stay where I am and close the door. Right ho, Mr Wilson.

Jones crosses to the door.
WILSON   Quietly.
He slams the door.
JONES   What?
There is a creaking sound which gets louder, then a terrific crash as the wall collapses.
They are all crouched on the floor. Clouds of dust cover them.
WILSON   I'm afraid he didn't close it quietly, sir.
HODGES   This is a nice mess you've landed us in, Mainwaring.
MAINWARING   Shut up!
Mainwaring and Walker rush over to the door. They try to open it.
WALKER   It's no use, Mr Mainwaring. There must be a ton of bricks up against that door.
MAINWARING   We're trapped!
FRAZER   Ay, doomed. Doomed!
Jones's face appears at the grille.
JONES   Permission to speak, sir. I'm afraid I closed the door a bit too hard.
MAINWARING (*at grille*)   Now listen carefully, Jones. I want you to go to the Command Post and find Private Sponge and tell them to come and rescue us.
JONES   Get help. Right ho, sir. Don't panic. Don't panic.
Pike is standing by the bunk.
WALKER   Captain Mainwaring, Mr Godfrey's waking up.
MAINWARING   What?
He rushes over to the bunk.
GODFREY   Oh hello. I'm afraid I must have dozed off for a minute.

WALKER Dozed off. He's been asleep for four hours.

MAINWARING What do you think you're playing at, Godfrey?

GODFREY Well sir, I haven't been sleeping too well lately, so when I was at the clinic this morning, they gave me some tablets. They must have been stronger than I thought.

MAINWARING How dare you take sleeping pills on active service! I've a good mind to. . . .

Jones's face appears at the grille.

JONES Permission to worry you, sir. I can't get out.

MAINWARING What!

JONES I went to open the other door and the handle's come off.

There is a long pause.

FRAZER I knew it—we're doomed! Doomed!

MAINWARING Be quiet, Frazer! I'm trying to think.

JONES (*shouting through grille*) Don't worry, Mr Mainwaring, you'll get an idea in a minute.

Mainwaring draws Wilson away from the others.

MAINWARING Quiet, Jones. Out of the way, Frazer. Keep calm, men. Now listen, Wilson, we've got to keep these men cheerful until help arrives.

WILSON Very well, sir.

MAINWARING Now whatever I do, you back me up and keep smiling.

WILSON You mean like this?

He forces a sickly grin.

MAINWARING I suppose that's better than nothing. Now pay attention, men. We're in a pretty tight spot, but it's only a matter of time before Private Sponge and the others realise we're missing and come looking for us. Meanwhile to keep our spirits up, we'll have a sing-song.

WALKER I'll give you one, Mr Mainwaring. (*Sings*) 'Twas Christmas Day in the Workhouse, and the candles had just been lit. . .'

MAINWARING No Walker, we want something that we can do actions to.

WALKER Well you can do actions to that.

MAINWARING Not those sort of actions. Something cheerful.

PIKE I've got an idea, sir. Why don't we do one of those camp fire songs we used to have in the boy scouts?

MAINWARING Excellent, Pike. We'll do 'Underneath the Spreading Chestnut Tree.' Wilson will do the cheerful actions, and you follow.

FRAZER If Sergeant Wilson is going to do cheerful actions, I'd rather be miserable.

MAINWARING I don't want any insubordinations, Frazer. Now, are you all ready?

He quickly crosses to Wilson.

MAINWARING I suppose you do know the actions, Wilson?

WILSON Well I think I saw it once on the 'Movietone News'.

MAINWARING Good. Sergeant Wilson will show you the actions.

WILSON I don't remember them awfully well. Wouldn't it be better if somebody else showed them?

MAINWARING (*taking him aside*) Now look here, Wilson. Back me up. Do the actions. That's an order.

WILSON Yes, sir.

MAINWARING Cheerfully.

They all sing. Wilson does the actions.

OMNES Under the spreading ... (*Wilson stretches arms overhead*)
Chest ... (*Strikes chest*) Nut ... (*Taps head*) Tree. (*Spreads arms*)
Where I held ... (*Embraces himself*) You on my knee. (*Strikes knee*)
There we raised a family, (*Scowls and emits a growl*) 'Neath the spread-
ing ... (*Arms outstretched*) Chest ... (*Strikes chest*) Nut ... (*Taps
head*) Tree.

MAINWARING Now we'll try it all together.

GODFREY Excuse me, sir. Do you want me to come down and join
in, or stay up here and join in?

MAINWARING Stay where you are, Godfrey. Jones.

JONES Yes, sir.

MAINWARING Don't forget to do the actions.

JONES You've no need to worry, sir. I shall do the actions. Even
though you cannot see me, sir, I shall do them to the hilt.

MAINWARING Right now, all together, with actions.

*They all sing with actions. On the last 'Chestnut Tree' Jones's face disap-
pears and there is a loud crash.*

MAINWARING Jones, Jones! Are you all right?

Jones's face appears.

JONES I fell off the chair, sir. It's difficult to do the actions pressed
up against the wall.

MAINWARING Just do the words, Jones. Right, once again.

They all sing.

*Cut to close-up of Pike, who is looking uncomfortable. Cut to pipe behind
him. Water is pouring out of several large cracks and one jet, stronger
than all the others, is shooting out and hitting Pike in the small of the
back. The song finishes.*

PIKE Mr Mainwaring, I feel all cold and wet.

HODGES Blimey! Look—water's coming out of the pipe.

FRAZER That bomb must have cracked it.

They all clear back from the pipe.

WILSON Perhaps, if we wrapped something round the pipe, that
might stop the flow.

MAINWARING Good idea. Pike, take your blouse off and wrap it
round the pipe.

PIKE Why me?

MAINWARING Because you're already wet. Now do as you're told.

HODGES What are we going to do if we can't stop it?

MAINWARING There is no such thing as can't, Hodges. Get in there,
boy, and wrap it round the pipe.

*Pike dives in and wraps his blouse round the pipe. The others retreat back
to the bunk.*

PIKE I don't think it's going to work.

FRAZER Stick at it, laddie, you're doing fine.

MAINWARING Hold your tongue, Frazer. I'll do any encouraging
there is to be done.

WILSON I've just remembered, sir. There are a lot of stopcocks in
the other room. Perhaps Jones could turn the water off.

MAINWARING Good thinking. Walker, tell Jones to try and turn
the water off by the stopcocks.

Walker jumps up on the bath.

WALKER Right ho! (*He shouts through the grille*) Hey, Jonesey!
We're being flooded out. Mr Mainwaring says try and turn the water
off.

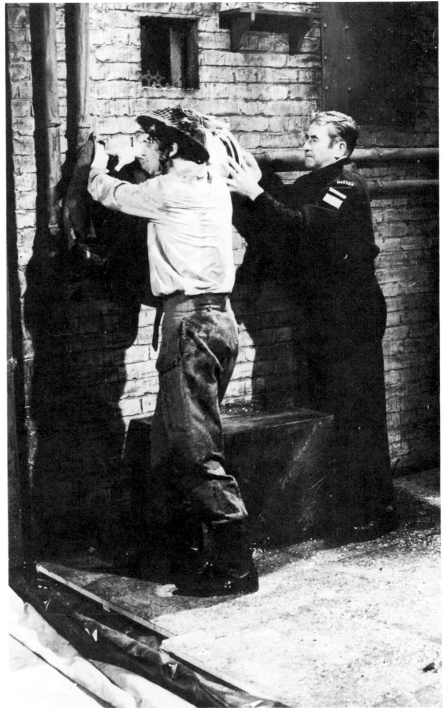

JONES   How can I do that?

WALKER   Turn the stopcocks.

JONES   What stopcocks?

WALKER (*to Mainwaring*)   What stopcocks?

MAINWARING   The stopcocks on the pipes.

WALKER (*to Jones*)   The stopcocks on the pipes, cock.

MAINWARING   This is no time for stupid jokes, Walker. Tell him to get on with it.

Jones stands in front of the stopcocks, scratching his head.

JONES   I wonder which way is 'off'.

WALKER   Hurry up, Jonesey. We're getting wet.

JONES   Which way is 'off', Joe?

WALKER   Which way is 'off'?

MAINWARING   Anti-clockwise.

WALKER   Anti-clockwise.

JONES (*looking at watch*)   Anti-clockwise. That means that way. No it doesn't, it means that way. (*He frantically turns the cocks*) Yes, that's right, that way, it must be that way.

Later that night. Mainwaring, Wilson, Frazer and Walker are clinging to the bunk. Hodges is standing in the tin bath. Water is coming through cracks in the second pipe as well as the first.

FRAZER   The silly old fool. He's making it worse.

Suddenly the first pipe comes apart at the 'S' bend and water gushes out.

WALKER (*shouting*)   You're turning it the wrong way, Jonesey.

The second pipe comes apart at the 'S' bend as well. They all shout 'Turn it off'. Jones is still turning the stopcocks.

JONES   Don't panic. Don't panic! I'll get it . . . I'll get it.

The water in the second room is now so deep that Mainwaring, Wilson, Frazer, Walker and Godfrey are crouching on the top bunk. Hodges is sitting in the tin bath, which is floating. Only Pike remains in the middle of the room. The water is pouring out of the two pipes. The level is just above Pike's knees.

PIKE   Mr Mainwaring, can I come up on the bunk please?

MAINWARING   I'm sorry, Pike, there's no more room.

PIKE   What am I going to do when it reaches my head?

MAINWARING   Don't worry, Pike. We'll have thought of something by then.

PIKE   Can I get in your bath please, Mr Hodges?

HODGES   No you can't get in my bath. There's only room for one. Stop mucking about and making waves. The slightest movement will have it over.

WALKER   I know, let's have a sing-song. How about 'Asleep in the Deep'?

They all give Walker a terrible glare.

Still later, the water has now reached Pike's chest. The rest are still on top of the bunk and Hodges is in the bath.

PIKE   Uncle Arthur. If you don't let me up on the bunk, I shall tell Mum.

WILSON   Oh do stop moaning, Frank. You can see there's no room.

PIKE   We haven't got much time left, Mr Mainwaring. You said you'd think of something before the water reached my head.

MAINWARING   We are thinking, Pike. (*To Wilson*) Have you thought of anything yet, Wilson?

WILSON   No, sir, but I'm working on it.

FRAZER   The water's getting higher and higher.

GODFREY   Perhaps it would be a good idea if we didn't talk very much, then we won't use up the air.

MAINWARING   Be quiet, Godfrey. If it hadn't been for you we wouldn't be in this mess in the first place.

FRAZER   We're entombed, entombed. I mind the time when I was a boy on the Isle of Barra. A submarine sunk in the bay. Seven brave men were trapped in it and the water rose higher and higher until, in the end, it came up to their necks. A terrible way to die.

HODGES   Oh, put a sock in it.

GODFREY   Mr Mainwaring, I wonder if I might. . . .

MAINWARING   If you want to be excused, it's impossible.

PIKE   I agree.

GODFREY   What I was going to say was, I think I've found a way out.

MAINWARING   Don't be absurd.

GODFREY   Here, sir.

He pulls aside the pillows, to reveal the manhole cover.

MAINWARING   And just how do you suggest that we undo the bolts?

WALKER (*pointing to spanners*)   Look, Mr Mainwaring, that's what the spanners are for.

MAINWARING   By Jove, I think you're right. Pike, get that large spanner.

WILSON   How awfully clever of you, Godfrey.

PIKE   I can't reach it, sir.

MAINWARING   Hodges, get that spanner.

HODGES   Mr Hodges to you, Napoleon.

MAINWARING   I presume you want to get out of here.

HODGES   Oh, all right. (*He takes his steel helmet off and paddles the bath to below the tool rack. He reaches out for the spanner*) I can't quite reach.

WILSON   Well, stand up.

Hodges gingerly stands up and gets the spanner.

HODGES   If I'm not careful I shall. . . .

He falls back into the water.

WALKER   Fall in!

Hodges stands up in the water. He has dropped the spanner.

MAINWARING   You've dropped it—of all the bungling, incompetent. . . .

PIKE   I'll get it, Mr Mainwaring.

Pike dives under the water and comes up with the spanner.

WILSON   Well done, Frank.

WALKER   Give it to me, Pikey.

Walker grabs the spanner and gets to work on the bolts.

MAINWARING   Can you manage it?

WALKER   A bit stiff, but it's coming.

In the first room, Jones is still wrestling with a stopcock.

JONES   I've got to close it. No use—it won't budge. I need something to lever it. (*He looks round*) One of these spanners will do. (*He rushes over to the tool rack, climbs up on the bench and grabs the spanner. His other hand is on the manhole cover, which he notices for the first time*) Blimey! Why didn't I think of that before? (*He fixes the spanner on one of the bolts*) It fits! (*He starts to unscrew the bolts and shouts*) Don't worry, my brave lads; I'll get you out of there. I'll rescue you!

Back in the second room, Mainwaring and Wilson are the only ones left on the bunk. The rest have gone through the hole. Pike and Hodges are standing in the water, holding on to the bunk.

PIKE   Give me a hand up, Uncle Sergeant.

WILSON   Don't get up here yet, Frank, you'll make us all wet.

HODGES   I'd like to make you wet, mate.

MAINWARING   Don't stand there arguing, Wilson! Get through.

Wilson starts to crawl into the hole.

MAINWARING   Then we'll go round and let Jones out.

Jones is unscrewing the last bolt.

JONES   I'm coming boys, I'm coming. (*He pulls the cover off*) Hold on, brave lads. Hold on! (*Eventually his head appears in the manhole connecting the first and second rooms*) It's all right boys, I've saved you. I've saved . . . (*He looks round. The room is empty except for seven steel helmets floating on the water*) Oh, no! Mr Mainwaring. Mr Mainwaring! Are you there, sir?

He reaches right through the hole and starts feeling around in the water. The door opens in the first room and Mainwaring, Wilson, Frazer, Walker, Godfrey, Pike and Hodges dash in. The door closes behind them.

MAINWARING   It's all right, Jones, we're here.

WILSON   He's gone.

FRAZER   No he hasn't. Look!

He points to Jones legs poking through the hole. They rush to the hole and pull Jones back into the room.

JONES   Oh thank goodness, Mr Mainwaring. I thought you were all drowned. I'm so pleased to see you.

MAINWARING   Come on, I've had enough of this. Let's get out of here.

He crosses to the door. It won't open.

MAINWARING   Who shut this door?

GODFREY   Well, it was rather draughty and I didn't want any of you to catch cold.

MAINWARING   There's no handle. You've done it again.

JONES   How are we going to get out?

MAINWARING (*slowly*)   One of us has got to get through that hole, into the room, and out through the other hole. And then go round and open this door. Whoever it is, is going to get very wet. Right, Wilson, take your trousers off!

Captain Mainwaring

CAPTAIN GEORGE MAINWARING is often quoted as saying that his father kept a tailor's shop in the best part of Eastbourne, and was a member of The Master Tailors' Guild. However, according to Jones, who is the only one who remembers Eastbourne at that time, Mainwaring's father in fact kept a small gents' outfitters in a side street, with old workmen's trousers hanging up outside. In spite of his humble background, he was determined to be someone, and by application and hard work he managed to gain a scholarship to the local Grammar School. When he left in 1902, he toyed with the vain hope that he might become a soldier. It had been a dream of his since childhood, but in those days a Grammar School education was hardly a fitting background for an officer and a gentleman. Besides, he had no money. He took up a position in Martin's Bank where, after twelve years' hard work, he became Assistant Chief Clerk.

When the war broke out in 1914, he at once volunteered. At last he was going to be a soldier, and be able to wear on his chest those medals which he had craved for all his life. But he was turned down because of his eyesight. During the next few years he made repeated attempts to join up and at last, thanks once more to his determination, he was commissioned as a 2nd Lieutenant in the Pioneer Corps. Mainwaring arrived in France on 14 November 1918, forty-eight hours after the Armistice, just too late to get any medals.

In 1919, with his hopes of glory dashed, he returned to civilian life, where he met and married Elizabeth, a large girl, who helped her sister to run a small wool shop. In later life he often wondered if she herself was in fact knitted, instead of flesh and blood—there was no issue from the union. He threw himself into his work, and in 1935 his ambition was achieved when he was promoted to Manager of

Martin's Bank, Walmington-on-Sea. At the age of fifty-five it seemed that his dreams of serving his country on active service were past. However, fate took a hand, and when in 1940 the Nazi invasion of these islands threatened, he grasped his opportunity with both hands, and formed the Walmington-on-Sea Local Defence Volunteers (later to become the Home Guard). By his efforts he welded them into a crack fighting force. At last, he had found his true destiny. But as we know the Germans never came, and alas, there were no medals for Mainwaring.

ARTHUR LOWE

Arthur Lowe feels a strong attachment to the sea, and as a boy wanted to be a sailor. He was turned down by the Navy because his eyesight wasn't good enough, but in 1938 joined the Army as a trooper. He spent some of his Army life in South Wales at the time when that area was under heavy bomb attack, trained with Radio Locations, and was then posted to the Middle East with R.E.M.E. to work on searchlight repairs. He became a sergeant-major, was very involved with Forces Entertainment, and returned from Egypt in 1945.

He spent many years touring in rep as a character actor, then made his West End debut in 'Larger Than Life' at the Duke of Yorks theatre. Other stage appearances include 'Call Me Madam', 'Pal Joey', 'The Pyjama Game', 'Inadmissable Evidence' and, more recently, the role of Stephano in 'The Tempest' at the National Theatre. He has also made many films, notably 'The Ruling Class', 'The Sporting Life', 'If', 'The Bed Sitting Room', and 'O Lucky Man', for which he received the SFTA Award for the Best Supporting Performance.

Other television work has included Leonard Swindley in 'Coronation Street' and Mr Micawber in 'David Copperfield'. Arthur Lowe sees a certain similarity between Swindley, Micawber and Mainwaring—each of them being a hopeless mess!

The Deadly Attachment

The platoon are drawn up on parade. They are all wearing full equipment and have their rifles with them. Mainwaring and Wilson are in front.

MAINWARING Now, pay attention, men. I have just received a new directive from G.H.Q. regarding Nazi parachutists, and I'll read it to you. (*Reading*) 'There is a danger that Home Guards might confuse British pilots and air crews who are bailing out, with actual German parachute troops. Not that our chaps get shot down very often, of course, but it can happen. A good point to remember here is the fact that no British plane contains more than six men. So if you see a bunch of parachutists floating down, you count them, and if there are more than six, you shoot them in the air.'

PIKE Mr Mainwaring, supposing they're dressed as nuns. Do we still count them?

MAINWARING You count them, however they're dressed. On the other hand, it's hardly likely that a whole plane-load of real nuns would drop by parachute.

JONES You never know, sir. I look at it this way. Supposing some-

where in occupied France there is a nunnery. And one day the chief nun calls all the other nuns together and she says, 'Look girls, I've had enough of being under Nazi heels, let us escape to dear old England,' and they all creep out and steal a plane. And they fly, and fly and fly. And when these flying nuns get here, they don't know how to land, so they all jump out by parachute.

MAINWARING   I think you're getting into the realms of fantasy now, Jones.

JONES   But it is a possibility, sir. It is a possibility.

MAINWARING   It's a million to one chance. But I suppose we should take every precaution.

WILSON   Excuse me, sir. If I may be allowed to interject at this point of the discussion?

MAINWARING   Hmmm?

WILSON   It's really perfectly simple, you see. As they float down, the turbulence of the air will cause the habits to rise and we shall be able to see their legs. Then we can tell if they're real nuns or not.

MAINWARING   A very good point, Wilson. That's it, look at their legs.

GODFREY   I don't think I should care to look at nuns' legs, sir. It would be very impolite.

MAINWARING   You'd just have to force yourself, Godfrey. This is war.

PIKE   Mr Mainwaring, I don't know what real nuns' legs look like. I've never seen them.

WALKER   If it comes to that, I don't think anybody has.

FRAZER   Hairy ones!

MAINWARING   I beg your pardon, Frazer?

FRAZER   If they're Nazis, they'll have nasty hairy legs with jackboots on.

WALKER   What do we do if the real nuns have got hairy legs with jackboots on?

MAINWARING   That will do Walker. Now. (*Reads*) 'If a Nazi parachutist is floating down with his hands up, would you think this was strange?'

WALKER   Not half as strange as if he was floating up with his hands down.

MAINWARING   I shan't tell you again, Walker. If he is floating down with his hands up, this does not necessarily mean that he is surrendering. He could have a grenade concealed in each hand, so watch it. (*The phone rings*) Answer the phone, Pike.

PIKE   Yes, Mr Mainwaring.

He crosses to the office.

MAINWARING   By the way, Wilson, while we're on the subject of grenades, have you primed our stock of Mills bombs?

WILSON   No, sir.

MAINWARING   I told you to do it yesterday.

WILSON   But it's awfully dangerous, sir.

MAINWARING   *War* is awfully dangerous, Wilson. What would you do if a hoard of Nazi parachutists were to descend on the Church Hall? Say, 'Wait a minute while we prime our grenades?' I want those bombs ready for instant use. See to it tonight.

WILSON   Yes, sir.

PIKE   (*returning*)   You're wanted on the phone, Mr Mainwaring. G.H.Q. It's very urgent.

MAINWARING   Thank you. (*He crosses to the door*) Take over, Wilson.

Mainwaring goes into the office, crosses to the desk and picks up the phone. The Colonel is on the other end, and we see a policeman standing behind him.

MAINWARING   Good evening, sir. Pike! Shut the door. No, the other side, boy.

COLONEL   Good evening, Mainwaring. I've got a very important job for you to do.

MAINWARING   Excellent. What is it, sir?

COLONEL   I've just had a message from the police. A fishing boat has picked up a U-Boat Captain and seven members of the crew. They're down at the harbour now, locked in the hold.

MAINWARING   By Jove, that's good news.

COLONEL   I want you to pick them up and take them back to the Church Hall. I'll send an armed escort over to collect them.

MAINWARING   Face to face with the enemy at last, eh, sir? Don't worry, we'll take good care of them.

COLONEL   They won't give you much trouble. They've been drifting at sea for two days in a rubber dinghy. Good luck.

MAINWARING   Thank you, sir. (*He hangs up, strides to the door and opens it*) Good news, men. After all these months of waiting, we're finally going to get to grips with the enemy.

WALKER (*to Jones*)   Blimey, don't tell me we're going to invade France.

Wilson hurries over to Mainwaring.

WILSON   You're not going to do anything hasty, are you, sir?

MAINWARING   I've got something very important to say to the men.

33

WILSON   Have you found out what nuns' legs look like?
MAINWARING   All right, Wilson. (*To men*) A fishing boat has picked up a U-Boat crew, and we're going down to the harbour to collect them.
JONES   We're going to collect a U-Boat crew. Right, fix bayonets. (*He rushes over to Mainwaring, waving his bayonet*) I can't wait to get at 'em, Mr Mainwaring. I just can't wait.
MAINWARING   Put that bayonet away, Jones. There's plenty of time for that when we get there.
JONES   I can't help it, sir. When I get a whiff of action, I reach for my bayonet. It's second nature, I tell you, second nature.
MAINWARING   Fall the men in outside.
JONES   Yes sir, yes sir. Fall in outside to collect a U-Boat crew. Rifles and bayonets at the double.
MAINWARING   Wilson, Pike. Wilson, while we're gone, I want you and Pike to prime all the grenades.
WILSON   If you insist, sir.
MAINWARING   I want it done by the time I get back. Right men, get a move on.
He follows the men out.

Later that night in the office, we see seven Mills bombs laid out in a row on the desk. Wilson and Pike are standing behind the desk. Pike has a bomb in his hand.

PIKE   O.K. youse guys, dis is a showdown. Share this pineapple amongst you.
WILSON   For goodness sake, put that down, Frank.
PIKE   Those Chicago gangsters used to call them pineapples, Uncle Arthur. I saw it in that film *Scarface* with Paul Muni.
WILSON   I don't care what they called them, they're very dangerous.
PIKE   These are quite safe, they haven't got detonators in. Shall I get them? *He goes to move.*
WILSON   Stay where you are, Frank, and don't do anything. I'll get the detonators. *He crosses to the cupboard and gingerly takes out a box.*
WILSON   This is so risky. (*He opens the box*) There's only two in this box.
PIKE   There's some more boxes at the back of the cupboard. Shall I . . .
WILSON   I don't want you to touch them, Frank. (*He pulls a box from the back of the cupboard and looks at the label*) Hmm. Dummy primers for training purposes only.
PIKE   We don't want dummy detonators, they're no good. There's a box of real ones at the back.
He reaches into the cupboard. Wilson stops him.
WILSON   Wait a minute, Frank. Look, er . . . um, how would it be if we were to put these dummies in the grenades, instead of the real thing?
PIKE   But Mr Mainwaring said we had to have them ready for instant action. What would we do if the Germans came?
WILSON   We could soon change them round, it wouldn't take a moment. We could get it done before the bells had stopped ringing.
PIKE   Mr Mainwaring will be awfully cross if he finds out.
WILSON   Yes, but somehow I can't help thinking he'll be even more cross if we all get blown up.
They move to the desk.

34

The Church Hall, the next day.
JONES   Left, right. Left, right.
Mainwaring, Walker, Frazer and Godfrey enter, followed by the U-Boat Captain and seven sailors. The rest of the platoon bring up the rear with fixed bayonets. Jones is milling around waving his bayonet at the prisoners, who have their hands on their heads.
JONES   Hande hoch! Hande hoch! Keep those Handeys Hock!
MAINWARING   All right, Jones. They can put their hands down.
JONES   Right. Handeys down, handeys down.
MAINWARING   All right, Jones.
JONES   But they're not Hock.
MAINWARING   Frazer, get the Lewis gun and set it up on the stage, so that it has a clear sweep of the entire hall.
FRAZER   Ay, ay, sir.
He goes into the office.
MAINWARING   Sponge, Hancock. Go and get a stepladder.
SPONGE   Right you are, Mr Mainwaring.
MAINWARING   Jones, get those prisoners into a tight group in the middle of the hall.

JONES   Yes sir. (*To prisoners*) At the double in a tight huddle. Into the middle of the hall. Move!
Jones and the rest of the platoon push the prisoners into a tight group in the middle of the hall. Wilson and Pike come out of the office.
WILSON   You got back then, sir. Did they give you any trouble?
MAINWARING   Not really. (*He lowers his voice*) But they're an ugly mob. You see that Captain? You want to watch him. He's a surly brute. He's done nothing but sneer and smoke cigarettes.
WILSON   I wonder if he's got any to spare. I'm right out of them.
MAINWARING   This isn't a cocktail party, Wilson. Did you prime those grenades?
PIKE   Well, Mr Mainwaring, we . . .
WILSON   I think I can honestly say, sir, that all the grenades now have detonators in them.

MAINWARING   Good. Pike, get the Tommy gun.

PIKE   Yes, Mr Mainwaring.

He goes into the office. Jones comes over to Mainwaring and Wilson.

JONES   The prisoners are now in a huddle in the middle of the hall, sir.

MAINWARING   Thank you, Jones.

Walker is talking to one of the sailors.

WALKER   'Ere, listen. Tell your mates that I am in the market for purchasing Nazi daggers, swastikas, badges, signed pictures of Hitler or similar souvenirs. I'll give you a good price.

The sailor shakes his head.

WALKER   Oh blimey, you don't speak English, do you? Look, Nazi daggers, see, daggers.

He makes a stabbing motion at the sailor, who jumps back. The Captain crosses to Walker.

CAPTAIN   Get away from my men at once.

WALKER   Don't start on me, mate.

MAINWARING   Come over here, Walker.

Walker crosses to Mainwaring, Wilson and Jones, who are standing in a tight group away from the prisoners.

MAINWARING   How dare you fraternise with the enemy?

WALKER   I was only asking them if there was anything they needed.

MAINWARING   I'll attend to that. (*He lowers his voice*) Now listen. The armed escort will be here shortly to collect these prisoners. Meanwhile we want maximum security, Wilson, maximum security.

WILSON   Yes, sir. Maximum security.

Frazer comes out of the office with the Lewis gun.

JONES   Wherer!

FRAZER   Here you are, sir. It's all loaded and ready.

MAINWARING   Right, set it up.

Frazer crosses to the stage, puts the Lewis gun on a card table and sits behind it.

JONES   Permission to speak, sir. How about cutting their trouser buttons off?

MAINWARING   What?

During this speech the Captain moves up quietly behind Jones.

JONES   Well, sir, if we cut their trouser buttons off, and they try to run away, it will show at once that they are something unusual. Then a person walking along the street, nonchalant like, will see these men running, with their trousers round their ankles, and they will investigate.

CAPTAIN   You!

JONES   What?

CAPTAIN   You don't dare to do anything of the sort. The Geneva Convention clearly states that prisoners of war will not be put in humiliating positions.

Jones gestures with his bayonet.

JONES   You'll be in a humiliating position, mate, if you get this up you.

CAPTAIN   Don't threaten me, you silly old fool.

JONES   I'm not . . .

MAINWARING   Jones. Jones! That will do, Jones. (*To Captain*) Go back into the middle and speak when you're spoken to.

WALKER   Yeah, get back into the huddle.

Pike comes out of the office with the Tommy gun.

CAPTAIN   I'm warning you, Captain.

MAINWARING   Just do as you're told. You see the sort of insolent swine we're up against, Wilson?

WILSON   Yes, sir. He has got rather an abrupt manner. But you must make allowances for him, he's probably upset because we sunk his submarine.

SPONGE   Where do you want this stepladder, Mr Mainwaring?

MAINWARING   Set it up by the door. Pike, get up there with your Tommy gun, then you've got a view of the entire hall.

PIKE   You know I don't like going up ladders, Mr Mainwaring, with my vertigo.

MAINWARING   Get up there at once, boy!

Pike starts to go up the ladder.

PIKE   It's ever so wobbly.

MAINWARING   Get up!

PIKE   I've got a note from the doctor.

MAINWARING   Do as you're told. Godfrey—where's Godfrey?

Godfrey is dozing in a chair by the door.

MAINWARING   Godfrey!

Godfrey wakes up.

GODFREY   Did you call, sir? (*He comes over*) I'm sorry, I must have dozed off.

MAINWARING   Dozed off! Here we are guarding a dangerous gang of cut-throats and you doze off. You're supposed to watch him like a hawk, like a hawk. Hold the ladder.

GODFREY   Yes, sir.

He holds the ladder. The phone rings.

MAINWARING   Take charge, Wilson.

He goes into the office, crosses to the desk and picks up the phone.

COLONEL   G.H.Q. here. Everything all right, Mainwaring?

MAINWARING   Yes, sir. I've got the prisoners safe and sound. They're all ready for you to pick up.

COLONEL   I'm afraid the escort won't be able to get over there until tomorrow morning.

MAINWARING   Do you mean to say that we've got to look after them all night?

COLONEL   Sorry, can't do anything about it. Just give them a blanket each and bed them down. And give them something to eat, of course.

MAINWARING   But we've only got our own sandwiches, Colonel.

COLONEL   Well, send out for some fish and chips.

MAINWARING   Send out for . . . .

COLONEL   I'll see that you get the money back. Be over about eight in the morning. Cheerio.

Mainwaring hangs up.

MAINWARING   Fish and chips! (*He quickly strides to the door and opens it*) Wilson, Jones.

WILSON   Yes, sir.

MAINWARING   The escort can't get over until the morning. They've got to be here all night.

JONES   In that case, I really think we ought to cut their trouser buttons off, sir. (*He drags out his bayonet*) Let me do it, let me do it, sir.

MAINWARING   Put that away, Jones. I shall have a word with the prisoners, Wilson.

WILSON   But you don't speak German.

MAINWARING   Oh, they'll know by the tone of my voice who's in charge. Believe me, Wilson, they recognise authority.

He crosses to the prisoners, followed by Wilson and Jones.

MAINWARING   Right now, pay attention.

The prisoners all come smartly to attention.

WILSON   They're awfully well disciplined, sir.

MAINWARING   Nothing of the sort. It's a slavish blind obedience. Not like the cheerful, light-hearted discipline that you get with our Jolly Jack Tars. I tell you they're a nation of unthinking automatons, led by a lunatic who looks like Charlie Chaplin.

CAPTAIN   How dare you compare our glorious leader with that non-Aryan clown! (*He takes out a notebook and pencil and writes*) I am making a note of your insults, Captain. Your name will go on the list and when we win the war, you will be brought to account.

MAINWARING   You can put down what you like. You're not going to win this war.

CAPTAIN   Oh yes we are.

MAINWARING   Oh no you're not.

CAPTAIN   Oh yes we are.

PIKE (*sings*)   Whistle while you work.
                Hitler is a twerp,
                He's half barmy,
                So's his army.

The Captain crosses to the ladder. The words die on Pike's lips.

PIKE   Whistle . . .

CAPTAIN   Your name will also go on the list. What is it?

Mainwaring crosses over, followed by Wilson.

MAINWARING Don't tell him, Pike.

CAPTAIN Pike. Thank you.

MAINWARING (*boiling*) Now look here. I've had just about enough. Tell your men from me that they're going to be here all night and they'd better behave themselves. Now get on with it.

The Captain shrugs his shoulders.

PIKE (*to Wilson*) Uncle Arthur. I don't think it's fair that my name should be on the list. I was only joking.

WILSON You should be more careful, Frank. You know that the Germans haven't got a sense of humour.

PIKE But you've said much worse things about Hitler. He's said much worse things.

WILSON Quiet, Frank, he'll hear you.

PIKE Do you think if you talked to him nicely, he'd take my name off the list?

During this, the Captain is speaking to the prisoners in German.

MAINWARING Have you told them what I said?

CAPTAIN Yes.

MAINWARING Walker!

WALKER Yes, Captain Mainwaring.

MAINWARING Is the fish and chip shop still open?

WALKER I think so. Why?

Mainwaring hands him a ten shilling note.

MAINWARING Go and get some for the prisoners. Jones, Wilson, a conference.

He walks over to Wilson and Jones.

WALKER (*to Captain*) Right. Eight cod and chips.

CAPTAIN I want plaice.

WALKER Right. Seven cod, one plaice. Who wants vinegar?

CAPTAIN (*in German*) Who wants vinegar?

Four hold up their hands.

WALKER Right. Four vinegar. Salt?

CAPTAIN (*in German*) Who wants salt?

Three hold up hands.

WALKER That's three salt. How many without salt and vinegar?

CAPTAIN (*in German*) How many without salt and vinegar?

More hands.

WALKER Two without. Now let's see if I've got this right.

MAINWARING (*approaching*) What do you think you're doing, Walker?

WALKER I was just taking the order.

CAPTAIN And I don't want nasty, soggy chips. I want mine crisp and light brown.

MAINWARING How dare you? Now listen to me. I've had just about enough. You'll have what you're given and if I say you'll eat soggy chips, you'll eat soggy chips.

Later that night. Jones is sitting behind the Lewis gun on the stage. Walker and Frazer are sitting beside him. Wilson is sitting in front of the stage, reading 'Picture Post'. Pike is up the ladder with the Tommy gun. Godfrey is sitting on a chair holding the ladder. Mainwaring is walking up and down, watching the prisoners, who are sitting on benches in the middle of the hall. The rest of the platoon are sitting in a circle round the

prisoners. The Captain is smoking and following Mainwaring with his eyes all the time.

FRAZER Fancy giving those Germans fish and chips. All I've had to eat tonight is paste sandwiches.

JONES You've got to treat prisoners of war properly, you know, Jock. I shall never forget when we was in the Sudan, we had a young officer, Captain D'Arcy Holdane his name was, and he used to say, 'Boys, always treat them Dervish prisoners well. See that they get plenty of betel-nut. If we treat them well, they'll learn by our example and treat us well.' Anyhow, a few days later he was captured.

WALKER What happened to him?

JONES They chopped his head off.

FRAZER Look at the time. One o'clock in the morning. You'd think he'd let some of us take it in turns to sleep.

WALKER It's no use, Taff. Captain Mainwaring won't let us take our eyes off them. He's obsessed.

Mainwaring is still walking up and down. Godfrey stops him as he passes.

GODFREY Do you think I could possibly be excused, sir?

MAINWARING Certainly not. Stick to your post.

PIKE Yes, don't let go of the ladder, Mr Godfrey.

Mainwaring walks back towards the stage. He stops when he gets level with the Captain, who is watching him like a hawk. He moves and turns again, and waves his hand at the Captain.

MAINWARING Don't keep staring at me all the time. Can't you look in another direction? (*He walks towards the stage and as he passes Wilson, he pokes him*) Put that down, Wilson. I told you to watch the prisoners. (*He goes up on stage*) Keep them well covered, Jones.

JONES   Don't you worry, sir. I'm watching 'em.

FRAZER   Yon Captain never takes his eyes off you for a minute, Mr Mainwaring. If you were to ask my opinion, I don't think he likes you very much.

WALKER   I wouldn't want to be in your shoes, sir, if he were to turn the tables on us.

MAINWARING   There's not much chance of that, Walker.

Hodges and the Verger enter the Church Hall office by the back door.

HODGES   Well I've had a good night tonight. I've booked three houses for showing lights and we've shared a bottle together, Mr Yeatman.

VERGER   By the way, Mr Hodges. Not a word to his Reverence that I keep a bottle in my hidey hole.

HODGES   You can rely on me. I'm the soul of discretion. Mum's the word. Better go and say goodnight to Napoleon.

Hodges and the Verger enter the hall.

HODGES   Good night, Napoleon. (*He sees the prisoners*) Blimey, what's all this?

MAINWARING   They're Nazi prisoners of war. Keep away from them.

VERGER   You've no right to keep Germans in the Church Hall. The Vicar will be furious.

MAINWARING   Mind your own business.

The Captain suddenly clutches his stomach and groans.

HODGES   What's the matter with you, mate?

CAPTAIN   I feel so ill.

He groans and slips to the floor.

CAPTAIN   It's my stomach.

HODGES   Give me a hand, Verger.

They both cross to the Captain.

MAINWARING   Come away from those prisoners at once!

HODGES   What are you talking about? Can't you see the man's sick?

The Captain is groaning and rolling on the floor.

FRAZER   He looks bad to me, sir.

WALKER   Perhaps it was them soggy chips you made him eat.

Mainwaring crosses down to Wilson.

WILSON   I really think we ought to do something, sir.

MAINWARING   I don't trust him, Wilson.

WILSON   We can't just leave him lying there.

HODGES   Well, don't stand there, Mainwaring. Do something. He's somebody's son, you know.

VERGER   He's got a heart of stone, you know, Mr Hodges.

GODFREY   There's some bicarbonate of soda in my red cross pack if that will help.

MAINWARING   Stay where you are, Godfrey.

PIKE   Yes, don't let go of the ladder, Mr Godfrey.

MAINWARING   Keep them well covered, Jones. Watch them like a hawk.

JONES   Yes, sir. Like a hawk.

MAINWARING   And you, Pike. I'm going in.

Frazer and Walker come down from the stage with their rifles and bayonets. Mainwaring crosses to the Captain, who is cradled in Hodges's arms. The Captain gives another groan and passes out.

MAINWARING   There's something funny here.

HODGES   What are you afraid of? They're only a few harmless German soldiers.

Mainwaring kneels over the Captain.

MAINWARING   He seems to be breathing all right.

Suddenly the Captain grabs Mainwaring's revolver, gets his arm round Hodges's neck and presses the revolver against it.

CAPTAIN   No one move!

MAINWARING   You, you . . . .

CAPTAIN (*in German*)   Get the machine gun!

42   *Two sailors advance on Jones, who picks up the Lewis gun and backs away.*

JONES   You're not having it. Stand back. Get back.

WILSON   Please be careful, Jonesey.

The two sailors jump up on the stage. Jones backs away, trips, the Lewis gun goes off and blows a hole in the roof. Pike falls off the ladder. Everyone dives for the floor as clouds of dust and bits of roof fall down.

Later that same evening. Mainwaring and the platoon are standing in a tight group in the middle of the hall, facing the door of the office. Jones is squatting behind the Lewis gun, which is on the card table. Frazer and Walker and Pike are standing beside him with rifles and bayonets. The rest of the platoon are grouped round them, except Sponge, Desmond and Hancock. They all have fixed bayonets. Godfrey is hovering in the background. Mainwaring is in the middle with the Tommy gun. All weapons are pointed at the office door. Wilson comes in from the main doors.

MAINWARING   Everything all right, Wilson?

WILSON   Yes, sir. I've posted Sponge, Hancock and Desmond outside. They've got the back door and window of the office covered.

MAINWARING   That stupid drunken fool Hodges!

JONES   I didn't let them have the gun, did I, Captain Mainwaring?

MAINWARING   You behaved very well, Jones.

JONES   I haven't felt like that since I was in the trenches in 1916 . . . I did do well, didn't I, Mr Wilson?

WILSON   You did awfully well, Jonesey.

JONES   You behaved well as well. You were very cool.

WILSON   Thank you.

FRAZER   When they've quite finished this mutual admiration society, perhaps you'd like to tell us what we're going to do now, Captain Mainwaring?

WALKER   Yeah, we can't stand here all night.

MAINWARING   They've only got one revolver, and they can't get out of the office. Believe me, Walker, we hold all the trump cards.

The office door opens a few inches. They all cock their rifles. A hand comes round the door and waves a white handkerchief. It is the Verger.

MAINWARING   Are they surrendering, Verger?

VERGER   No. I've got a message from the Captain. He says he wants you to take him and his men back to the fishing boat, so that they can cross to France.

MAINWARING   What!

VERGER   If you don't agree to his terms, he's going to blow Mr Hodges's head off.

JONES   We can't let them escape, sir. If they get back to France, they could get another submarine and start sinking our ships again.

WILSON   Jones is right, I'm afraid, sir.

WALKER   It's one man's life against thousands.
FRAZER   A terrible decision you've got to make, Captain Mainwaring. But, you must admit, you've never liked the man.
MAINWARING   Tell him we need time to think it over.
VERGER   Right.
He hurries back to the office. Inside the office Hodges is sitting at the desk. The Captain is standing beside him with the revolver stuck in Hodges's neck. The rest of the sailors are standing round. The Verger comes in.
CAPTAIN   Well?
VERGER   He's thinking it over.
CAPTAIN   I'll give him until dawn.
HODGES   What did Mainwaring say?
VERGER   I must admit, Mr Hodges, it doesn't look too good for you.
HODGES   Oh no!

In the Church Hall, Mainwaring, Wilson, Jones, Frazer, Walker, Godfrey and Pike are sitting in a group. The rest of the platoon are standing round.
WALKER   If only we could get that gun away from him somehow.
JONES   Permission to speak, sir. I have an idea. Supposing I was to put on some old clothes, black my face, knock on the door and say I am a chimney sweep? And when I see Mr Hodges, I will say, 'Hello Fritz.' And they will say, 'Why do you call him Fritz?' And I will say, 'Because he is not British, he is a German prisoner of war, who works

as an A.R.P. Warden in his spare time.'

MAINWARING   Please, Jones.

JONES   But it will sow the seeds of doubt in their minds, sir. And while the seeds are being sown, I will jump on the Captain, and if the gun goes off, it might not hit Mr Hodges.

Mainwaring gives Jones a look of despair.

PIKE   Mr Mainwaring. I saw a film called the *Petrified Forest*. And Humphrey Bogart was holding Leslie Howard by gun point in a cabin all night. And Leslie Howard kept quoting poetry and using long words. And it didn't half upset Humphrey Bogart. Perhaps you could do the same, sir.

WILSON   I missed that film. What happened to Leslie Howard in the end?

PIKE   He got shot.

MAINWARING   You stupid boy.

GODFREY   I saw Freddie Bartholemew in *David Copperfield*, sir. But there wasn't really anything in that.

MAINWARING   Oh, all the . . . wait a minute. *David Copperfield*! Mr Micawber, 'Something's bound to turn up.' That's it. We'll play along with them. We've got to go through the town to get to the harbour, someone's bound to raise the alarm. (*He shouts at the office*) All right, we agree to your terms. (*To Wilson*) Even if they get to the boat, Wilson, the Navy will blow them out of the water before they've gone a mile.

The office door opens and the Captain, with Hodges at gunpoint, comes out of the office. The Verger and the rest of the sailors follow.

CAPTAIN   I'm glad you have come to your senses, Captain. (*In German to one of the sailors*) Get the machine gun. Cover them.

The sailor covers them with the Lewis gun.

CAPTAIN   (*to platoon*) Put your rifles down.

They hesitate.

MAINWARING   Put them down, men.

They pile their rifles on the floor.

CAPTAIN   Get me a grenade and a piece of string.

MAINWARING   Do as he says, Wilson.

WILSON   Yes, sir.

He goes into the office.

CAPTAIN (*to the sailors, in German*)   Unload the rifles, take the bayonets off.

They unload the rifles.

MAINWARING   You won't get away with this. We're bound to be spotted going through the town.

CAPTAIN   No one will interfere, Captain, because you will be escorting us with empty rifles.

MAINWARING   And how are you going to make us do that?

Wilson returns with a Mills bomb and a piece of string.

CAPTAIN   Very simply.

He hands the revolver to one of the sailors, who holds it against Hodges's neck. He takes the bomb and string from Wilson.

CAPTAIN   Is it primed?

WILSON   Oh yes.

The Captain unscrews the base plug.

CAPTAIN   You don't mind if I make sure?

WILSON   By all means.

The Captain looks in the bomb.

CAPTAIN   Good. (*He screws back the base and then speaks to Jones*) You, old man, take off your belt and undo the back of your tunic.

JONES   I beg your pardon?

CAPTAIN   Do as I say. Remove your belt.

He ties the end of the string to the ring of the pin. Jones takes off his belt and unbuttons the back of his blouse.

CAPTAIN   Just to make sure that your behaviour is correct, Captain, the old man will march in front of me . . . (*He puts the bomb in the waist band of Jones's trousers*) One false move from you and I pull the string.

He buttons up the back of Jones's blouse.

JONES   Don't make any false moves, Mr Mainwaring, or even real ones.

CAPTAIN   Seven seconds will give me plenty of time to get clear, but I think it is not enough time for the old man to unbutton his tunic.

FRAZER   A terrible way to die.

MAINWARING   You unspeakable swine. Now listen to me. I'm the Commanding Officer here, it's only right that I should have the bomb in my waistband.

JONES   I will not allow you to have a bomb in your trousers, sir. Don't you worry about me, they can put twenty bombs in my trousers. They won't make me crack.

MAINWARING   How can you hope to beat us? You see the sort of men we breed in this country?

CAPTAIN   Yes, rather stupid ones.

MAINWARING   You can sneer, but you've forgotten one thing, Captain.

CAPTAIN   What is that?

MAINWARING   The Royal Navy. You've got to cross twenty-five miles of water. You'll never make it.

CAPTAIN   I think we will, because all of you will be on the boat with us. (*He points to Godfrey*) We shall leave the old man behind, to tell them. Your Navy won't fire on their own people. (*He takes Mainwaring's revolver, empties it and puts it back in the holster*) So, when we get to France, you will be my prisoners, and then we shall examine the list.

The next day. We see the procession marching along. Mainwaring is in front, the Captain is close behind him with the rest of the sailors. They are surrounded by Frazer, Jones, Walker and Godfrey and the rest of the platoon carrying rifles. Wilson and Pike are in the rear. Hodges and the Verger are marching level with Mainwaring.

PIKE   Uncle Arthur. If I tell the German there's a dummy detonator in the grenade, do you think he'll take my name off the list?

WILSON   Be quiet, Frank!

The Colonel comes round the corner.

WALKER   Blimey, sir! Look, it's the Colonel.

MAINWARING (*over his shoulder to the Captain*)   The game's up now. What are you going to do?

CAPTAIN   I am not going to do anything. You will bluff your way out.

MAINWARING   I refuse to co-operate in any way whatsoever.

JONES   Please, Mr Mainwaring, if you don't do as he says, he'll pull the string.

MAINWARING   Oh no he won't.

CAPTAIN   Oh yes I will.

JONES   He says he will, Mr Mainwaring.

They draw level with the Colonel.

MAINWARING   Platoon halt!

COLONEL   Where on earth are you taking the prisoners, Mainwaring?

MAINWARING   The fact is sir, I . . .

WALKER   We're going for a walk, sir. Captain Mainwaring thought it would be a good idea if we gave them some exercise. They've been cooped up in a submarine for weeks.

COLONEL   What on earth's the matter with you, Mainwaring? You're as white as a sheet. You look as if you've seen a ghost.

FRAZER   Breath of fresh air will do him the world of good, sir.

GODFREY   We're just going down to the harbour. These sailors like a sea breeze.

COLONEL   Oh, all right then. I'm on my way to the railway station to pick up the escort for the prisoners. See you later.

MAINWARING   Yes sir, yes sir. Platoon by the right, quick march!

They start to move.

COLONEL   Wait a minute! Halt!

They halt.

COLONEL   You know, I'm surprised at you, Mainwaring. Your men are usually so smartly turned out. Why isn't Jones wearing equipment? And what's that great lump of string hanging down his back?

MAINWARING   Where?

COLONEL   Here.

He pulls the string and holds it up. We see the pin on the end of it.

MAINWARING   Oh no!

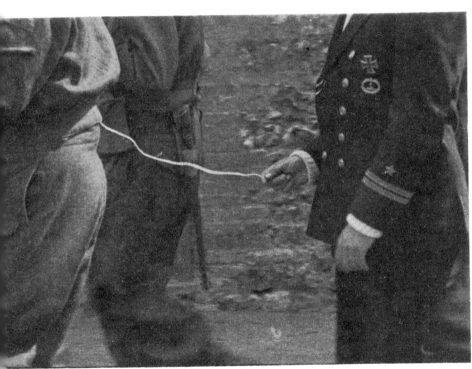

Everyone except the Colonel, Jones, Wilson and Pike dive for cover and flatten themselves against the ground.

JONES   I've got a bomb in my trousers. Don't panic! Don't panic!

MAINWARING   Get it out, Jones.

He starts to unbutton the back of his blouse. Hodges is holding the Verger, who has his fingers in his ears.

FRAZER   I'll get it, sir. I'll get it.

JONES   It's slipped down, Mr Mainwaring.

WALKER   Hang on, I'll cut it out.

Frazer thrusts his arm down the back of Jones's trousers.

JONES   Save yourself, Mr Mainwaring.

Wilson crosses to the Colonel.

WILSON   I wonder if I might borrow your revolver, sir.

Mainwaring and Jones are dancing in the road.

JONES   Don't panic, sir. Don't panic, sir.

COLONEL   What the hell's going on?

WILSON   I'll explain later. (*He waves the revolver at the prisoners*) Now listen to me, you German chaps. Would you mind just getting up against the wall, with your hands up please.
The prisoners obey.
MAINWARING   Jones, wait a minute. It should have gone off by now.
They both stop.
JONES   So it should. I've been saved, sir. I've been saved.
Mainwaring crosses to Wilson.
MAINWARING   I thought I told you to prime those grenades.
WILSON   I did, sir. With dummies.
MAINWARING   Why is it you will never . . . You've saved Jones's life, Wilson.
WILSON   Now perhaps you'll agree with me, that it's awfully dangerous to keep them primed.
JONES   Now that the crisis is past, Mr Mainwaring, would you mind asking Private Frazer to take his arm out of my trousers?

Sergeant Wilson

JOHN LE MESURIER

Born in Bedford, John le Mesurier abandoned a career in law to follow a long-nurtured desire to be on the stage. He studied at the Faye Compton School of Acting, then spent the pre-war years touring in rep. Called up at the outbreak of World War II, he finished his service as a captain on the northwest Indian frontier.

Back in England, he began to do a lot of work in the cinema, and has now made close to two hundred films, including 'Only Two Can Play', 'The Pink Panther', 'The Liquidator', 'Casino Royale', 'Doctor in Trouble', and 'Brief Encounter'. He is also well known for his many television appearances, and in 1971 won the Best Television Actor Award for his leading role in Dennis Potter's play 'Traitor'.

SERGEANT ARTHUR WILSON is one of those reticent people who rarely open their hearts to their fellow men. For this reason he has remained something of a man of mystery. He was born in 1887 in a rambling country house in Gloucestershire. His great uncle, a peer of the realm, entered him at birth for Harrow, but unfortunately the boy failed his Common Entrance exam. A lesser public school readily accepted him, the headmaster being another great uncle. Young Arthur was destined for the Indian Civil Service and having failed that exam it was a toss up whether he would go into the army or a merchant bank. The great uncle with the merchant bank lost the toss so the City had the advantage of Arthur's early years.

He soon became a legend, not so much for his skill with banking, as his skill with bankers' daughters, and publicans' daughters—in fact, any daughters. He served in the army from 1915 to 1918 and would undoubtedly have been commissioned had he not failed to turn up at the selection board owing to the breakdown of a chorus girl's alarm clock.

In the post-war years he returned to banking and in the mid-twenties married one of Mr Cochrane's Young Ladies. She left him not long after the birth of their only child, a daughter, who is currently serving in the WRENS. In the mid-thirties while working at Martin's Bank in Weston-super-Mare, he met Mrs Pike who, to his surprise, followed him to Walmington-on-Sea when he was appointed Chief Clerk at Mr Mainwaring's branch. He is on the list for promotion to Branch Manager but his rise above that position is unlikely. Arthur Wilson has run out of time—and great uncles.

The Godiva Affair

The Church Hall. Mainwaring is talking to Private Hancock, who has a rifle and a fixed bayonet.

MAINWARING Right, Hancock, you are to stay on guard outside this door and let no one through. Understand?

HANCOCK Right, sir. Let no one through.

MAINWARING Maximum security. Is that clear? Maximum security?

HANCOCK Yes, Captain Mainwaring, maximum security.

Mainwaring goes through the door into the hall.

MAINWARING Right, men, this is top secret. Put the blackouts up. Private Woods and Meadows—on guard outside the main doors. No one is to enter. I don't care who they are.

Mainwaring knocks on the office door.

MAINWARING All clear out there, Hancock?

HANCOCK All clear, sir.

Mainwaring comes down to the centre of the hall.

MAINWARING All clear, Jones?

JONES (*from beneath the stage*) Right you are, sir.

The door at the side of the stage opens. Jones, Frazer, Pike and Godfrey, Cheeseman and Sponge file on. They are dressed as Morris Dancers.

MAINWARING   Excellent turn out, men. Excellent.

JONES   Permission to speak, sir. Aren't you going to put on your attire?

MAINWARING   Not at the moment. I'll just wear the hat. Now pay attention. The reason I have taken all these precautions to keep this a secret is because I don't want us to look like a bunch of idiots. (*He puts on the bowler hat with ribbons*) No one must see us until we get this dance perfect.

FRAZER   Captain Mainwaring, if I can have a word. As a Scot, I must say that I object to wearing these pansy sassernach clothes.

JONES   They are not pansy! This is our English national dress.

FRAZER   English national dress, rubbish! Cricket clothes, with bells and ribbons on.

MAINWARING   All right, Frazer, you can sneer, but if you care to work it out, it's a costume that sums up the English character pretty well. Clean white cricket flannels that stand for fair play and sportsmanship. The bowler hat that stands for respectability and clear thinking. And the ribbons and bells for just a touch of frivolity.

GODFREY   Beautifully put, Captain Mainwaring.

JONES   General Kitchener liked a touch of frivolity, sir. He used to wear great long. . .

MAINWARING   All right, Jones, we've no time for that now.

JONES   Pity, it was a good story.

MAINWARING (*shouts*)   Hurry up, Wilson!

WILSON   (*from beneath the stage*) Do you think that someone could open the door for me, sir?

MAINWARING   Go and help him, Pike. (*To the others*) Now I don't want to take too long over this rehearsal, we've got a full training programme ahead of us tonight. Private Day.

DAY   Yes, Captain Mainwaring.

MAINWARING   Stand by with your concertina.

DAY   Right.

Day plays a chord.

MAINWARING   Good.

Wilson comes through the door wearing a hobby horse with a skirt and little legs, which are the wrong way round. He has some trouble getting through the door.

WILSON   This is really most awkward, sir.

MAINWARING   You'll soon get used to it.

JONES   Permission to speak, sir. Sergeant Wilson is not looking like a normal man—his little legs are going in the wrong direction.

MAINWARING   Do try and sort yourself out, Wilson. As you know, men, we only need another two thousand pounds to reach our target, which is to buy a Spitfire. Now, during the whole of next week, everyone in Walmington-on-Sea will be doing their utmost to raise the money. The grand climax will be the procession next Saturday afternoon; that is when we will perform our dance. Sergeant Wilson will collect the money from the crowd.

WILSON   I don't think I like the idea of asking strangers for money.

MAINWARING   It's perfectly simple. All you have to do is to gallop the horse—try to make it look as life-like as possible—then you weave in and out of the dancers. Then you weave round the edge of the crowd, pull open the horse's mouth for them to put the money in, and while you're doing it, make jocular remarks.

WILSON   What sort of jocular remarks?

MAINWARING   Oh I don't know. You could say, 'Har, har har, give 'til it hurts. Har, har, har.' Try that.

WILSON (*pathetically*)   Har, har, har, give 'til it hurts. Har, har, har.

JONES   If we're going to collect two thousand pounds he'll have to be a bit more jocular than that, sir.

GODFREY   I don't think he can afford to be too jocular, otherwise people will think he's being over-familiar.

PIKE   I've got it. Why can't he say, 'We need Spitfires to beat the Hun, put money in my mouth and it goes to my tum.'

FRAZER   Rubbish. All he's got to do is to wave his stick at the crowd and shout, 'Give us some money or I'll bash you on the head.'

WILSON   Oh really, sir, couldn't you get someone else to do the horse?

MAINWARING   No, you are going to do the horse, and that is an order. Right. Form up. Sponge, give the book to Sergeant Wilson.

They form up in two lines facing each other. Frazer opposite Jones, Pike opposite Godfrey and Sponge opposite Cheeseman.

MAINWARING   Now where did we get to last time?

JONES   I was having trouble with my whiffling, sir.

MAINWARING   Oh yes. Whiffling. Now I think it is very important that we should fully understand the meaning of these movements. Read out the bit about whiffling, Wilson.

WILSON   Whiffling, whiffling. The movements with the whiffling stick represent frightening the evil spirits away.

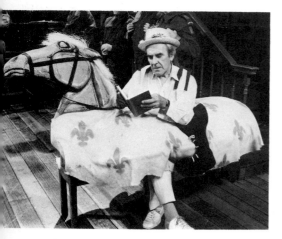

PIKE   Away from what, Mr Mainwaring?

MAINWARING   This is a fertility dance, Pike.

GODFREY   I don't think my sister Dolly would approve of that sort of thing, sir.

FRAZER   Ah, you silly old fool. The whole idea of this dance is to encourage the crops to grow. It's danced every Spring by the young fertile men of the village.

JONES   Well, there's not much point in us doing it.

FRAZER   You speak for yourself.

MAINWARING   All right, that will do.

JONES   Permission to speak, sir. I do not want to stand opposite Private Frazer when he is whiffling.

MAINWARING   Why not?

JONES   Well sir, I have faced whirling Dervishes, and I have faced charging Fuzzie Wuzzies, but I do not want to face Private Frazer when he is waving his whiffling stick. He has a mad look in his eyes.

FRAZER   Mad? Mad? My eyes are perfectly sane. Captain Mainwaring, would you say that I had mad eyes?

MAINWARING   Well, er. . .no. . .not really mad.

FRAZER   There you are.

MAINWARING   What's next, Wilson?

WILSON   The bean sprouting.

MAINWARING   Ah yes, the bean sprouting. Come here Pike. Now you tap twice on the ground, so . . . (*He taps Pike's stick*) Then you shout, 'Woa!' and leap up in the air; this represents the beans growing.

PIKE   How high do you want us to leap, Mr Mainwaring?

MAINWARING   As high as a bean grows.

CHEESEMAN   I had some last year that grew to eight feet.

GODFREY   I don't think I could quite manage that, sir.

SPONGE   I can leap high, Mr Mainwaring. How's this?

He shouts 'Woa!', gives a terrific leap in the air and lands with a crash.

MAINWARING   Yes, yes.

WILSON   I think we ought to be a bit careful, sir. The Vicar's got dry rot in the hall.

MAINWARING   Perhaps you're right, Wilson. We won't do the leap. Now we'll go through the whole thing from the start. Ready, Day?

DAY   Ready, sir.

He gives a blast on his concertina.

MAINWARING   Oh, just before we start. I'd better make sure that your bells are working properly. Left legs.

They all shake their left legs.
MAINWARING   Right legs.
They all shake their right legs.
MAINWARING   Can't you make any more noise than that, Godfrey?
GODFREY   A touch of rheumatics I'm afraid, sir.
Mainwaring gives Godfrey a look of despair.
MAINWARING   Right. Off we go.
JONES (*silent mime*)   One, two, three, four.
FRAZER   Five, six, seven, eight.
They move back. They move forwards. They circle clockwise. They circle anti-clockwise. They whiffle. They do bean sprouting. They whiffle again and finish.
MAINWARING   Excellent, men. I'm very proud of you. Right, now take a break and change into your uniforms. Jones.
JONES   Yes, sir.
Mainwaring takes him aside.
MAINWARING   Now look, Jones, what's the matter with you? All that nonsense about Frazer hitting you with his stick. That's not like you at all.
JONES   I know, sir. I'm afraid I cannot cover it up any longer. I am in a highly nervous state.
MAINWARING   What's the matter?
JONES   Well sir, it's er . . . (*he lowers his voice*) It's er, very personal.
MAINWARING   Have you got trouble at home?
JONES   No sir, I've got trouble away from home.
MAINWARING   You'd better come in the office.
JONES   Can Sergeant Wilson come as well, sir?
MAINWARING   Why?
JONES   'Cause he's a man of the world.
MAINWARING   Oh, very well. Wilson.
WILSON   Sir.
MAINWARING   Office.
WILSON   Do you want me to walk or gallop?
MAINWARING   Just get in the office!

56

Inside the office.
MAINWARING   Sit down, Jones.
JONES   Thank you, sir. Thank you.
He sits. Mainwaring sits behind the desk. Wilson stands at the top of the desk. The horse's head goes right across the desk.
MAINWARING   Now, Jones.
(*The horse's head blocks his view of Jones*) Get that thing off the desk, Wilson.
WILSON   I'm sorry, sir. I can't help it, it sort of sticks out.
MAINWARING   Well, take it off.
Wilson takes off the horse.

57

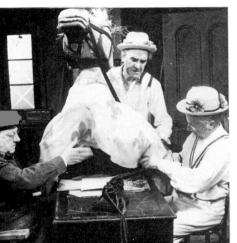

MAINWARING   Now come along, Jones.
JONES   This really is very delicate, sir, you see it's er . . . Mrs Fox.
MAINWARING   Mrs Fox?
JONES   Yes, sir. She's a widow lady and we both have a certain arrangement. For some time now we've been walking out.
MAINWARING   Walking out where?
JONES   All over the place. You see I take a couple of chops round to her house every Saturday night, she cooks them and we have supper together.
MAINWARING   I see. (*He looks at Wilson*) You're not the only member of this platoon who has that arrangement with a widow, Jones.
WILSON   Really, sir, that was a bit below the belt.
JONES   There is nothing between Mrs Fox and myself, sir. It is purely a tutonic arrangement. As I said, every Saturday night we have supper together, and listen to 'In Town Tonight'. Then when the announcer says, 'Carry on London,' I go home.
MAINWARING   I really don't see what this has got to do with me.
JONES   Well sir, just lately, her affections have been taken by another.
MAINWARING   Who?
JONES   Mr Gordon, the Town Clerk.
WILSON   What, that silly old, bald-headed duffer? (*He laughs and breaks off as Mainwaring gives him a glare*) I, er . . . don't mean that he's a silly old duffer because he's got a bald head. He'd be a silly old duffer even if he had a full head of hair.
MAINWARING   All right, Wilson. All right.
JONES   Everyone knows that he is a roué and a philanthropist. Her head has been turned by the gay life that he is showing her. Old Time dancing at Pevensey Bay, and trips into Eastbourne. What can I offer her? I'm just a simple butcher.
MAINWARING   But I really don't see what I can do, Jones.
JONES   I want you to speak to her for me.
MAINWARING   But I couldn't possibly. . .
JONES   You must, sir, you must. (*He rises and hands Mainwaring a piece of paper*) Here, I've written down her telephone number. Don't spread it around.
MAINWARING   Yes, but. . .
JONES   Please speak to her, sir. Otherwise I shall be a broken man, and what use is a broken Lance Corporal to you? (*He goes.*)
WILSON   What are you going to do, sir?
MAINWARING   I don't know. I suppose I could speak to her. I think perhaps I ought to point out what sort of a man this Town Clerk is. I'll give her a ring and arrange to meet her.

Frazer's house at night. Frazer is on the telephone. He is in his dressing gown.

FRAZER   Hullo, hullo, Godfrey, son, are you there?

Godfrey's cottage at night. Godfrey is also in his dressing gown.

GODFREY   Yes I'm here; I was just having my hot milk before going to bed.

FRAZER   Well it's happened. I knew it would some day.

GODFREY   What has?

FRAZER   Mainwaring has succumbed to the lure of the flesh. Did you hear what I said, Godfrey son? The flesh, the flesh!

GODFREY   Oh please don't keep repeating that word, my sister Dolly might hear you. Anyhow, I refuse to believe a word of it.

FRAZER   I tell you, I heard it with my own ears. It just so happened that I was passing the office door and I heard him speaking to this woman.

GODFREY   Er . . . what woman?

FRAZER   Mrs Fox. That fine big widow woman.

GODFREY   But Mr Mainwaring is a pillar of respectability.

FRAZER   It's men like him that are the worst. Always looking down his nose at other people, and all the time, inside, lust, lust, sheer naked lust. I tell you, the fires of hell are lying in wait for him. He's doomed. Doomed!

GODFREY   I think the whole thing's nonsense.

FRAZER   Nonsense, is it? I heard him arrange to meet this woman at the Marigold Tea Rooms tomorrow morning at ten-thirty. If you don't believe me, come and see for yourself.

GODFREY   Very well, I'll come. Just to prove that you're wrong.

FRAZER   Right, I'll see you there, and don't forget it's your turn to pay for the coffee.

A telephone box at night. Cheeseman is on the phone. He is in civilian clothes.

CHEESEMAN   Hullo, hullo. Listen Pikey, I've got to speak to you. It's very important, boyo.

Pike's house at night. Pike is on the other end of the line. He is in his pyjamas and dressing gown.

PIKE   What do you want to ring me up at this time of night for? Mum's furious.

MRS PIKE   Who's that on the phone, Frank? It's not a girl is it?

PIKE   No, Mum, it's Mr Cheeseman.

MRS PIKE   How dare he ring you up in the middle of the night? Tell him to go away.

PIKE   It's only ten o'clock, Mum.

MRS PIKE   I don't care. You should be in bed. And don't forget to clean your teeth.

PIKE   Mum says I've got to go to bed and clean my teeth.

CHEESEMAN   Oh yes. Clean your teeth. They're very important. I just want a bit of information. What time does Mainwaring go for his morning coffee?

PIKE   Ten-thirty every morning at the Marigold Tea Rooms, regular as clockwork. Why?

CHEESEMAN   Well, I have it from a very reliable source, that Captain Mainwaring is meeting a certain lady there.

PIKE Oh no, Mr Mainwaring doesn't know certain ladies, he's married.

CHEESEMAN Well she's not so much a lady, see, she's sort of . . . well you know, very much . . . (*He gestures with his hands*) Anyhow, I write this gossip column for the Eastbourne *Gazette*, 'Whispers from Walmington'. Oh yes, indeed, I can see it now. 'What certain local bank manager's name is linked with a mysterious widow lady?'

PIKE I'm sure you've got it all wrong.

CHEESEMAN My information is that he's besotted with this woman.

PIKE Hey, like in that film *Rain*. This clergyman was besotted with a girl called Sadie Thompson. Well, being a clergyman, he wasn't allowed to be besotted, so in the end he walked into the sea. Here, you don't think Captain Mainwaring will walk into the sea, do you? If he does, he'll have to walk miles. Tomorrow morning, the tide's out!

Interior of the Marigold Tea Rooms. Frazer and Godfrey are sitting at a table in the corner; they are both dressed in civilian clothes. Cheeseman is sitting at another table behind a newspaper, also in civilian clothes. There are two booths: Jones is sitting in one, behind a newspaper. He is wearing a balaclava, bowler hat and mac.

GODFREY I'm sorry Mr Frazer, Mr Mainwaring is a respectable married man. I refuse to believe that he's capable of such a thing.

FRAZER You know your trouble, Godfrey, you live in a fool's paradise. I tell you. . .

Mainwaring and Wilson enter.

FRAZER Whist. Here he is.

Mainwaring nods at Frazer and Godfrey.

MAINWARING I had hoped that we'd have the place to ourselves.

WILSON I shouldn't worry, sir. No one knows why you're meeting Mrs Fox.

60

MAINWARING   All the same, it doesn't do for a man in my position to be seen in a public place with a flashy woman like Mrs Fox. In a small town like this, tongues wag, you know, tongues wag.

WILSON   I'm sure no one's the slightest bit interested, sir. Where shall we sit?

MAINWARING   I shall sit here . . . (*He points to a booth*) You go and sit on your own.

JONES   Psst, psst! Mr Mainwaring.

MAINWARING   Good morning. Is that you, Jones?

JONES   You won't let me down, will you, sir?

MAINWARING   Why on earth are you dressed like that?

JONES   I'm in disguise, sir. I don't want anybody to recognise me.

Mrs Fox enters. Jones disappears.

MRS FOX   Yoo, hoo! Morning Mr Frazer, Mr Godfrey; morning Mr Wilson. (*They all react*) Hullo Mr Mainwaring. Sorry I'm late.

MAINWARING   Please sit down, Mrs Fox.

MRS FOX   I'm usually on time when I meet a gentleman friend, but today. . .

MAINWARING   Sit down, please.

He pushes her into the booth.

FRAZER   Did you see that, Godfrey! Did you see the way he handled her?

MRS FOX   (*settling down*) Well, this is cosy. . .

The waitress comes to the table.

WAITRESS   Good morning, sir.

MAINWARING   Ah, good morning. Two coffees, please.

WAITRESS   Aren't you having coffee with your friend Mr Wilson this morning?

MAINWARING   No, I'm having coffee with my er . . . this lady here.

WAITRESS   I see.

She giggles and goes. Pike comes in.

MAINWARING   Now Mrs Fox. I have er . . . asked you to meet me here today because. . . .

Pike's head comes over the top of the booth.

PIKE   Excuse me, Mr Mainwaring.

MAINWARING   What do you want, boy?

PIKE   Mrs Mainwaring's on the phone.

MAINWARING   What! Oh yes. Well, tell her I'll ring her back later.

PIKE   Ring her back later. Right. Hullo, Mrs Fox.

MRS FOX   Hullo, dear.

Pike goes.

MAINWARING   Well now, Mrs Fox. I've asked you to meet me here today, because I have to speak to you on a very delicate matter.

MRS FOX   (*leaning forward*) Yes?

MAINWARING   I find these things concerned with emotions very difficult to discuss.

MRS FOX   You needn't be shy with me, Mr Mainwaring.

MAINWARING   Well now the fact is, Mrs Fox, you are a very attractive woman. What I'm trying to say is, you have had Mr Jones as an admirer for some years, and now, of course, you have another.

MRS FOX   Oh, Mr Mainwaring.

She grabs his hand.

FRAZER   Did you see that! Did you see?

GODFREY   Oh dear. Perhaps we'd better go.

Cheeseman is writing, Wilson is looking. Mainwaring snatches his hand away.

MAINWARING   I realise, of course, that, being a public figure, this other man must seem very attractive to you.

MRS FOX   Oh, he does.

MAINWARING   Jones, on the other hand, is just a simple butcher, but a fine figure of a man, Mrs Fox. A full head of grey, distinguished hair. Your other admirer is, not to put too fine a point on it, bald.

MRS FOX   Well, you know what they say about bald-headed men, Mr Mainwaring.

MAINWARING   What do they say?

Pike comes in.

MAINWARING   The point is, Mrs Fox, Jones is a very loyal member of my platoon and I don't want him hurt.

MRS FOX   We won't hurt him, Mr Mainwaring.

MAINWARING   We!

MRS FOX   He can have Mondays and Saturdays, and you can have Tuesdays and Fridays.

MAINWARING   Madam, I'm talking about Mr Gordon, the Town Clerk.

MRS FOX   Well, he can have Wednesdays.

PIKE   Excuse, me, sir.

MAINWARING   What is it boy?

PIKE   Mrs Mainwaring is on the phone again. I told her you were busy having coffee with Mrs Fox, but she insists on speaking to you.

MAINWARING   You *stupid* boy!

Mainwaring's office.

MAINWARING   I tell you, Wilson, I've never had such a shock in all my life. That woman, that dreadful woman, actually thought that I had amorous intentions towards her.

WILSON   How awfully embarrassing for you, sir.

MAINWARING   And on top of everything, when my wife phoned up, that stupid boy Pike told her I was having coffee with Mrs Fox. There was hell to pay when I got home; Elizabeth refused to listen to my explanations, and look what she did to my tie. (*He pulls his tie out. It has been cut short at the ends*) She rang me up twelve times at the bank today. Now if she rings tonight, I want you to tell her I'm not here. You understand?

WILSON   Yes, all right, sir.

Jones comes in.

JONES   Evening Mr Wilson, evening sir. I want to thank you for speaking to Mrs Fox. I'm sure you had a great effect on her.

WILSON   Yes, he really did.

Frazer, Pike, Godfrey, Cheeseman and several other members of the platoon enter. Frazer is carrying the Lewis gun.

FRAZER   We can't get into the hall, sir, the doors are locked.

PIKE   Mr Hodges shouted at us to go away.

MAINWARING   As if I haven't got enough to put up with as it is.

He crosses to the office door. It is locked.

MAINWARING   It's locked, Wilson.

WILSON   It is Hodges's night to have the hall, sir.

MAINWARING   I know that, but there's no need for him to lock the door. All right, Frazer, put the Lewis gun on the desk. I'll start the lecture.

He crosses to the desk.

MAINWARING   Now my subject tonight, men, is stripping down.

The Church Hall. The Vicar, Verger and Town Clerk are sitting at a table in the middle of the hall. Hodges is standing by a hobby horse in front of the table.

HODGES   All right, girls, you can come out.

Five girls in swimming costumes come through the door at the side of the stage.

HODGES   Line up, girls.

They line up.

HODGES   Right. What do you think, Mr Town Clerk?

TOWN CLERK   Oh, they're very nice, they are.

VERGER   I quite agree with you. What do you think, Your Reverence?

VICAR   Look, can we get on please. I've got a very busy evening ahead of me.

Hodges crosses to the Vicar, nudges him and leers.

HODGES (*whispering*) I wouldn't mind having a busy evening with this lot, eh?

VICAR   Just explain to the girls what we want, Mr Hodges.

HODGES   Right. Now girls, as you know, we have got you here to-night so that we can choose one of you to play the part of Lady Godiva in the procession next week.

TOWN CLERK   Can we have the first girl on the horse, please?

HODGES   Right, girls. On the horse.

Girls move to the horse.

Meanwhile, in Mainwaring's office, Mainwaring and the rest of the platoon are gathered round the Lewis gun on the table. Pike and Wilson are by the door; Pike has his eye to the keyhole.

MAINWARING   Right, Jones, I want you to show the men how to strip the Lewis gun down in two minutes, and I shall time you. Are you ready?

JONES   Yes sir, yes sir.

MAINWARING *(looking at his watch)*   Strip.

Jones starts on the gun. Pike straightens up and whispers in Wilson's ear.

PIKE   Uncle Arthur, the hall's full of naked girls.

WILSON   Don't be stupid, Frank. Pay attention to the lecture.

PIKE   It's true, look for yourself.

He pushes Wilson down to the keyhole.

WILSON   Good heavens!

PIKE   Shall we tell Mr Mainwaring?

WILSON   Well I, er. . . .

The phone rings.

MAINWARING   Answer the phone, Sergeant.

WILSON   Yes, sir.

MAINWARING   Hurry up, Jones, you've only got another thirty seconds.

Wilson picks up the phone.

WILSON   Hullo. Oh good evening. Just a minute. (*He puts his hand over the mouthpiece and whispers to Mainwaring*) It's Mrs Mainwaring, sir.

MAINWARING   I told you to tell her I'm not here.

WILSON   Sorry, sir. (*Into the phone*) I'm afraid he's not here.

Mrs Fox suddenly appears.

MRS FOX *(in a loud voice)* Yoo hoo, Mr Mainwaring, I'm here.

MAINWARING   Oh, no!

He grabs the phone and hangs up.

MRS FOX   Sorry, just on my way to the hall. Excuse me, boys. (*She pushes her way through the crowd. She is carrying a small case. She knocks on the door*) Let me in Mr Gordon, I'm here.

64

Gordon opens the door.

TOWN CLERK   Good evening, my dear. You're just in time. Come in.

JONES (*agitated*) Mr Mainwaring! Mr Mainwaring! He's at it again; what's he doing?

MAINWARING   I'll soon find out.

He goes into the hall, followed by the others.

MAINWARING (*beside himself*)   What is the meaning of this?

HODGES   Buzz off, Napoleon, this is my night to have the hall.

MAINWARING   How dare you! How dare you have naked girls in my H.Q.? I'm appalled at you, Vicar. Don't keep staring at them. Cover them up. (*To Pike*) Come away, boy.

VICAR   Don't be absurd. All this fuss over a few silly girls.

VERGER   Yes, if the Vicar wants to have silly girls in his hall, that's his affair.

MRS FOX   Shall I change into my swimming costume now, Mr Gordon?

FRAZER   I don't think I could stand the shock.

TOWN CLERK   Yes, my dear. Go and get changed.

JONES   Mr Mainwaring, stop him! Stop him!

MAINWARING   Be quiet, Jones. I demand an explanation, Hodges.

HODGES   Keep your hair on, we're just choosing a girl to play the part of Lady Godiva in the procession next Saturday.

MAINWARING   Lady Godiva!

HODGES   Yes, and it's much better than your silly Morris Dancing.

JONES   Our Morris Dancing is not silly.

MAINWARING   Now, Town Clerk. Do I understand that one of those young ladies is going to ride . . . er . . . bare, through the streets of Walmington-on-Sea?

TOWN CLERK   Yes, it's a tribute to the brave City of Coventry; the girl won't be bare, of course. She'll wear fleshings.

MAINWARING   Fleshings!

WILSON   Yes, they're all-over body tights, and perfectly respectable.

MAINWARING   All-over body tights!

HODGES   Yes. Lovely. We're not living in Victorian times, you know.

TOWN CLERK   Now wait a minute, Captain Mainwaring, I think we have a solution. You don't want one of those young girls as Lady Godiva. Now it's just been pointed out to me that Lady Godiva Leofric was, in fact, a woman of more mature years. So in the course of historical accuracy, I suggest that Mrs Fox should be Lady Godiva.

Uproar from girls.

TOWN CLERK   Quiet, please! Mrs Fox will be perfectly respectable, covered from top to toe in fleshings, and wearing a wig of long golden tresses.

FRAZER   You'll never cover her with golden tresses. You'll need a bell tent.

Back in Mainwaring's office. Mainwaring is on the phone.

MAINWARING   Yes, Elizabeth . . . no, Elizabeth. I keep telling you I did *not* have anything to do with choosing Mrs Fox to play the part of Lady Godiva.

Wilson comes in.

MAINWARING   Yes, dear . . . no, dear. It was the Town Clerk's decision. He thought it would be better for the part to be taken by a woman of more mature . . . well ample proportions . . . yes, dear, I realise that you are more ample than Mrs Fox. But then, you're not Lady Godiva, are you . . . hullo, hullo, dear? (*He hangs up and gives Wilson a sickly grin*) Just chatting to the little woman.

WILSON   Oh, what little woman?

MAINWARING   My wife, of course.

Jones comes in.

JONES   I've lost her, Mr Mainwaring. Since the Town Clerk chose Mrs Fox for Lady Godiva, her head's been turned completely, right round.

WILSON   I'm sorry, Jonesey.

MAINWARING   This is what happens, Wilson, when women come into men's affairs. The whole platoon has been thrown completely sideways.

Pike and Mrs Pike come in.

PIKE   You can't come in now, Mum, we're just going to start the parade.

MRS PIKE   Get out of my way, Frank. (*She nods to Mainwaring*) Arthur, what's this I hear about Mrs Fox being chosen as Lady Godiva?

WILSON   It was really nothing to do with me, Mavis.

MRS PIKE   You were there.

WILSON   Well I was only sort of standing around.

MRS PIKE   A woman like Mrs Fox! I'm much slimmer than she is. I mean, what's wrong with my figure?

WILSON   Er, nothing.

MRS PIKE   And I've got nice legs, haven't I? Haven't I got nice legs?

WILSON   Yes, awfully nice.

MAINWARING   You wouldn't want to be Lady Godiva, Mrs Pike.

MRS PIKE   But I would have liked to have been asked.

MAINWARING   Now Mrs Pike, consider how your son here would have felt, seeing his mother riding through the streets, clad only in. . . .

PIKE   Fleshings.

MAINWARING   Well, I know how I would have felt if it had been anyone close to me. So my advice to you is to let sleeping dogs lie.

The next day in the Marigold Tea Rooms. Mainwaring and his men are waiting in the shop. All the blinds are down. They are dressed as Morris Dancers.

MAINWARING   Right men, are you all ready? Now as soon as the procession has gone past, Jones will open the door, we will burst out of the tea rooms into the street and perform the dance.

GODFREY   I'm not awfully good at bursting out of tea rooms, Mr Mainwaring.

MAINWARING   You'll just have to do the best you can, Godfrey.

Sound of a band and crowds cheering. Pike pulls the blind aside.

PIKE   Here comes the procession now.

MAINWARING   Good. Stand by.

Mrs Fox bursts in. She is wearing a coat and her hair is all over the place.

JONES   Mrs Fox. What's happened?

MRS FOX   (*in tears*) It was terrible, terrible.

JONES   Now don't you upset yourself. (*He puts his arm round her*) There, there, you're safe with your little Jack. Just tell me what's the matter.

The music gets louder.

MAINWARING   There's no time for all that, Jones.

MRS FOX (*sobbing*)   I was going to change in a room in the Town Hall, and I left my fleshings and wig on a chair. Well, I went out for a minute and when I got back they were gone. Gone!

FRAZER   So it doesn't look as if we're going to get a Lady Godiva after all.

MAINWARING   Never mind, it's up to us now. (*He pulls Jones away from comforting Mrs Fox*) That's enough of that, Jones. Get ready to open the door.

He pushes Jones towards the door. Pike pulls the blind aside.

PIKE   Hey, Mr Mainwaring, there is a Lady Godiva.

WILSON   Oh Lord, not Mavis.

Mainwaring pushes to the door.

MAINWARING   You really should keep that woman under control, Wilson.

JONES   No, Mr Mainwaring, don't look, sir, please don't look.

MAINWARING   Get out of the way, Jones.

Mainwaring pulls the blind to one side and looks. He gives a low moan and faints into Jones's arms.

PIKE   Hey, it's Mrs Mainwaring!

Jones cradles Mainwaring in his arms.

JONES   Speak to me sir, speak to me. Poor Mr Mainwaring, he'll never get over it.

FRAZER   Ay, and neither will the horse.

Lance Corporal Jones

CLIVE DUNN

Clive Dunn comes from a family with a strong show business history, starting with his grandfather, comic Frank Lynn. He had already established himself as an entertainer when war broke out and he joined the Fourth Hussars as a trooper. His regiment was captured in Greece by the Germans, but he managed to slip away and spent some time on the run in the mountains. Eventually he was captured, shunted from compounds to labour camps, and spent three years, together with forty other men, in a two-room prison in Austria.

After the war his first big break came with ITV's 'Bootsie and Snudge', in which he played Old Johnson. Clive Dunn has been portraying old men virtually since he began on the stage, and his record 'Grandad' reached number one in the charts. He was recently awarded the OBE.

After the Charge of the Light Brigade, when a handful of the tattered survivors had staggered back to the British lines, and as Lord Cardigan and Lord Raglan were arguing as to whose fault it was, a ragged scarecrow of a Private soldier stepped forward and saluted. His once brave uniform was covered in the grime of battle. 'Permission to speak,' he said. 'Shall we go again, sir?' These few words sum up the bravery of the British N.C.O.s and Private soldiers who over the centuries have survived blunders and disasters, and have somehow always come out on top. Such a man is LANCE CORPORAL JACK JONES, born in 1870. At the age of fifteen he signed on as a drummer boy, and a few months later he was in the Sudan with Sir Garnet Wolseley's relief force, to save General Gordon who was besieged in Khartoum. Alas, they arrived two days too late. 'Permission to speak, sir,' said Jones. 'We should have come a bit quicker.' 'Nonsense, my man,' replied the Officer. 'We had to stop to water the horses. Besides, better late than never.'

Thirteen years later, Jones was again serving in the Sudan, this time with General Sir Herbert Kitchener, where at the Battle of Omdurman the Dervishes were finally beaten. 'Permission to speak, sir,' said Jones. 'We gave 'em the old cold steel, they don't like it up 'em.'

'That's the sort of fighting talk I like to hear,' said General Kitchener. 'Stick with me and you won't go wrong.' So Jones served with the General in India on the North West Frontier, and in France in 1914. When the war was finally over Jones hung up his uniform, and opened a small butcher's shop in Walmington-on-Sea. He thought his soldiering days were over, but when in 1940 England was once again threatened he didn't hesitate. At the age of seventy, he joined the Home Guard. 'Permission to speak, sir,' said Jones. 'I may be old but I can still give them the old cold steel, and they don't like it up 'em, you know, they do not like it.'

Everybody's Trucking

Jones's van is parked outside the Church Hall and Jones, Frazer, Godfrey, Pike and the platoon are standing by it waiting for Mainwaring. The van has been newly painted and is looking very smart.

PIKE It looks very posh, Mr Jones.

JONES Well you have to look after things these days, don't you, Pikey boy? I mean, they don't make vans like this any more. So you have to nurture them with craftmanship and oil and things. (*He points to the lettering*) That's real gold leaf, that is.

FRAZER Vanity, pure vanity. He just wants to bandy his name all over the town, like he was a tin of baked beans.

GODFREY I think it looks very jolly. It'll cheer people up as it goes along the road, even though there isn't any meat in it.

Mainwaring and Wilson enter from the door to the side office. Mainwaring is holding a clipboard.

MAINWARING Wilson, gather the men round with their secret signs. This is very confidential.

Mainwaring consults his clipboard. Wilson goes up to Godfrey and speaks very quietly to him.

WILSON   Would you mind gathering round Captain Mainwaring. (*He goes to a group and whispers*) Gather round Captain Mainwaring, please.
Wilson then goes to Pike and whispers in his ear. Mainwaring sees what's going on.
MAINWARING   Wilson.
Wilson moves behind the van to whisper to some of the platoon.
MAINWARING   Wilson! (*He crosses to the back of the van where Wilson was last seen*) Wilson, where are you?
Wilson appears round the front of the van.
WILSON   (*still whispering*) Did you want me, sir?
MAINWARING   What are you doing?
WILSON   You told me to gather the men round confidentially.
MAINWARING   Look. (*He taps his clipboard*) What I have to *say* is confidential. Not the fact that they have to gather round.
WILSON   I'm sorry, sir.
MAINWARING   Pay attention everybody.
PIKE   Excuse me, sir, Mr Jones has just had his van done up. Don't you think it looks nice?
MAINWARING   Don't interrupt, Pike, or you'll be sent home. Now, what I'm about to say is very highly confidential.
WILSON   It does really look awfully nice.
MAINWARING   I beg your pardon?
WILSON   Jones's van. He's made a marvellous job of it, hasn't he?
MAINWARING (*looking*)   Yes. Now this area has been selected. . . .
PIKE (*interrupting*)   Will Sergeant Wilson get sent home if he interrupts any more?

MAINWARING   I shan't tell you again, Pike. As I was saying, this area has been selected for the divisional scheme and the broad plan is as follows.

He puts his foot on the running board of the van to rest the clipboard on his knee, while turning over a page. As he does so, the running board falls off.

JONES   Mr Mainwaring, you've broken my running board.

He goes to put it back.

MAINWARING   Leave it where it is. We'll deal with it later.

JONES   You shouldn't have done that, Mr Mainwaring.

MAINWARING   Do be quiet and go back to your place, Jones.

JONES (*to platoon*)   He put his great heavy leg on it.

PIKE   Better be quiet Mr Jones, or he'll send you home. He's in one of his moods.

MAINWARING   Three batallions of regular troops will move into this area around Walmington and Eastgate and will defend it in depth. Our task is a vitally important one. We are to signpost the area so the units reach their correct destinations. (*He takes a piece of chalk from his clipboard*) Now the axis of advance is down the Clayton Road, thus.

He chalks a vertical line down the side of Jones's van, across the lettering.

JONES   Don't do that, Mr Mainwaring.

MAINWARING   Don't fuss, Jones. It'll soon come off.

He licks his finger and rubs. Some of the lettering peels away.

JONES   You're making it worse, Mr Mainwaring.

Mainwaring rubs it with his cuff.

JONES   Please don't do that to my van, Mr Mainwaring, you're desecrating it.

MAINWARING   Oh, you can soon retouch that. Now, of course, all the signposts have been removed, so without our help the whole convoy could finish up in chaos. That is why you were told to prepare the secret signs to guide them. Now, who has the signpost for Walmington?

Pike holds up a wooden sign which says 'Walmington', and shows a hand with a pointing finger The hand is painted very realistically.

WILSON   That's very good, Frank. The hand is absolutely lifelike. Don't you think so, sir?

MAINWARING   Yes. Well done, Pike.

GODFREY   It has dirty finger nails. I don't like that sort of thing.

FRAZER   There's just one thing. It points the wrong way.

MAINWARING   What do you mean?

FRAZER   When you come down yon road, Walmington is to the left.

MAINWARING   Ah. I was wondering who would be the first to notice that.

PIKE   Well, that's easily solved, isn't it?

He turns the sign upside down.

MAINWARING   Stupid boy!

PIKE   All they have to do is stand on their heads, sir.

MAINWARING   Don't be impertinent, Pike.

JONES   It's very simple, sir. (*He takes the sign*) We put it up thus wise. (*He shows Mainwaring the blank side*) Now, a body of men, on seeing a sign with nothing on it, will find it intriguing and wonder to themselves if there's nothing on the other side as well. But when they come round the other side, it will point the right way and we will win the war.

MAINWARING   Where's the Eastgate one?

Godfrey holds up a sign on which is drawn a Chinaman, a gate, and an arrow.

GODFREY   Er, this is it, sir.

MAINWARING   What's that?

GODFREY   You said it was secret, so I did the thing in code. (*He points*) The Chinaman for 'east' and gate for 'gate'. Eastgate.

MAINWARING   It doesn't look much like a Chinaman to me. Anyway, it's not a very good idea, Godfrey.

PIKE   Send him home, Mr Mainwaring.

MAINWARING   Now, you will each be dropped off the van to fix your notice, and then, as soon as the convoy has passed, you will destroy it.

WILSON   Destroy the convoy?

Mainwaring gives him a killing look.

WILSON   Destroy the notice.

JONES   Do we have to eat it, sir?

GODFREY   I hope not. My new dentures are hardly up to it.

MAINWARING   You will destroy it by fire.

FRAZER   Suppose it's raining and they don't light?

MAINWARING   War is fraught with hazard, Frazer. Now you will be

dropped off the van, one by one, and I shall give the signal like this.

He raps the side of the van twice with his stick.

JONES   Mr Mainwaring, do you mind not striking my van in the aforesaid manner?

MAINWARING   Don't keep fussing, Jones. There's a war on, you know.

JONES   There's no need for you to spoil my van. That's up to Hitler, isn't it?

MAINWARING   Now it's quite on the cards that during the exercise you will have to take the van across country and, of course, we could get stuck. Now this is nothing to worry about, as long as we are pre-pared. Jones, get into the van and pretend you're driving along and then you get stuck.

JONES   You won't have to hit it again, will you, Mr Mainwaring?

MAINWARING   Get into the van, Jones.

Jones starts to climb in.

MAINWARING   Now, the sort of materials you should carry with you are, one—(*He points to these items, which are standing against the wall*) sawdust. Two—old sacks. Three—planks, and four—a length of rope. With these and a bit of brute force, you should be able to over-come any hazard. Right, Jones.

JONES   Dimmer, dimmer, dimmer, dimmer, dimmer. I'm driving along, sir. Dimmer, dimmer, dimmer, dimmer. Oh dear, I think I'm stuck. Whur, whur, whur.

MAINWARING   Good, Jones. Switch off. The wheels are spinning. What do we do?

FRAZER   Sawdust, sir, or straw, to give a grip. And, of course, a wee push.

MAINWARING   Good. Now take up your pushing positions.

The platoon move round to various positions around the van. Pike goes to the rear of the back wheel.

MAINWARING   I shall supervise from here.

He puts his hand on the side lamp in front of Jones. It comes loose in his hand.

JONES   Don't do that please, Mr Mainwaring, you've made it dangle.

MAINWARING   You really should look after your van better than this. It's falling to pieces. Get back in the van. Sawdust, Wilson.

WILSON   Pardon, sir?

MAINWARING   Sawdust, Wilson.

PIKE   Over there, Uncle.

WILSON   Well, what about it?

MAINWARING   Put it under the wheels, Wilson! And don't dawdle, Wilson. There's a lot of ground to cover.

Wilson sprinkles some near the wheel.

WILSON   Like this, sir?

MAINWARING   You need more than that, man.

Wilson pours the whole sackful on to the ground.

WILSON   Is that better?

MAINWARING   Good. That's much more like it. Clear it up, Pike.

PIKE   He just chucked it down.

MAINWARING   Do as you're told, boy. Now that will get you out of mud and soft ground and, of course, it'll do just as well if you throw down straw.

PIKE   He's not going to throw down straw, is he?

MAINWARING   Sacking will sometimes do the trick and, of course, one should always carry a few planks. Now there's one little wrinkle that's worth knowing, if you have to deal with a lot of ice. Lower the pressure of the rear tyres. Now this is very easily done. You merely. . . (*He begins to demonstrate*) push the valve needle down and allow a little air to escape.
He stands up. The air still hisses out.
JONES   Mr Mainwaring, what are you doing to my van?
MAINWARING   The valve's stuck, that's all. Give it a kick, Wilson.
Wilson kicks the tyre gently. The hiss continues.
MAINWARING   Not like that. The plunger needs shaking up.
Mainwaring gives the tyre a good kick. The hiss continues.
JONES   Mr Mainwaring, you're spoiling my van.
MAINWARING   By jove, it's a stubborn one.
He continues to kick. Frazer, Pike and the others start to join in, kicking the tyres and banging the sides.
JONES   Leave my van alone! Leave it alone! Go away, all of you!

A country road the next day. Jones's van is progressing along the country road. Mainwaring, Wilson and Jones are in the driving cab; Wilson is sitting between Mainwaring and Jones, who is driving. Frazer and Pike are looking through the trap.
MAINWARING   Right. First signposter stand by.
FRAZER   He's standing by, sir.
MAINWARING   Stand by to tick him off the list, Wilson. (*He turns to call through the hole*) Now this is a great honour and a great responsibility. One sign wrong and we could ruin the whole divisional scheme.
FRAZER   There's the turning.
MAINWARING   Right. Stop, Jones. First signposter out.
He bangs his stick twice on the side of the van.
JONES   Mr Mainwaring, please don't start spoiling my van again.
MAINWARING   Don't be absurd, Jones. I must give the signal to the men.
JONES   Couldn't you make some other sort of noise, sir? One that doesn't spoil my van?
PIKE   Why don't you toot your hooter?
MAINWARING   Good suggestion, Pike. (*He calls to the men at the back*) We'll toot the hooter when we want you to disembark. Is that clear?
FRAZER (*to back of van*)   He's going to toot his hooter when it's time.
PIKE   I get some good ideas sometimes, don't I?
GODFREY   Captain Mainwaring. The first man has alighted safely.
MAINWARING   Good. Drive on, Jones.
Later, along the road.
MAINWARING   Right, Jones, signal the last one out. Tick him off the list, Wilson.
Jones pushes the horn. Nothing happens.
JONES   Mr Mainwaring, the hooter isn't tooting.
MAINWARING   Give it a good hard push.
He leans across and bangs his hand on the horn. It sticks in the 'on' position. They bash it more. It falls off the note and slides down to silence.
JONES   You've broken my horn, Mr Mainwaring. If you go on like this, I won't have anything left.

MAINWARING Never mind, Jones, you're helping the war effort.

PIKE Mr Mainwaring, the last signposter has just dropped off the back.

MAINWARING Good. Turn round, Jones. We'll go back to the crossroads and wait for the convoy to pass through and then we can pick everybody up again.

Jones starts to turn the van.

They are on the return trip and are confronted with a steam roller and organ trailer which they are unable to pass.

MAINWARING *(from the van)* Get out of the way!

JONES It's been left alone and uncared for, sir.

MAINWARING We'll go and investigate.

Jones, Mainwaring and Wilson get out of the van. Pike and Frazer get out of the back and approach the steamroller.

WILSON There's nobody with it.

MAINWARING I can see that, Wilson.

PIKE Captain Mainwaring. Perhaps the driver's gone into a field to have a. . . .

MAINWARING That'll do, Pike.

FRAZER Captain Mainwaring, does it not put you in mind of the Marie Celeste? She was found abandoned in the midst of an empty ocean, food on the table, wine in the glass, not a human soul on board, dead or alive. Only the creaking of the rigging and the eerie cry of the birds. Cor! cor! Cor! cor! Does it not strike you, Captain Mainwaring? Do you not see the connection?

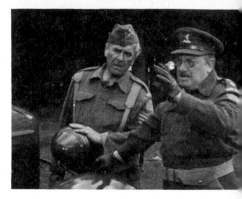

MAINWARING No, not really.

GODFREY Captain Mainwaring, there's a note here. *(He holds up the note)* It says, 'Gone to get some coal.'

MAINWARING Well, we can't wait here. He might have gone for miles. We'll drive round. Back in the van everyone.

WILSON *(as they go towards the van)* There's been rather a lot of rain lately, are you sure we won't bog down?

MAINWARING Nonsense, Wilson. The ground's as firm as a rock. Anyone can see that. Everybody on the van.

Mainwaring and Wilson start to climb into the van.

WILSON In that case, wouldn't it be wiser for us all to stay off the van, to lighten the load?

MAINWARING You're not very scientific, Wilson, are you? Anybody knows that extra weight gives more traction to the driving wheels. Do use your common sense. Drive on, Jones.

They drive off the road and around a phone box on to the field. The wheels spin. Jones struggles. Mainwaring looks worried. They stick.

PIKE *(from a hole in the roof)* Captain Mainwaring, we're stuck.

MAINWARING Right. Everybody off. Pushing positions.

They climb off.

WILSON *(as they climb off)* Do you think that some of them should stay on, so as to give more traction to the wheels, sir?

MAINWARING Don't be flippant, Wilson. And try not to look so miserable.

WILSON *(giving a wan smile)* Is that better?

FRAZER We're ready in our pushing positions, sir.

GODFREY Er, Captain Mainwaring. Would it be in order if I only push with one hand? I've a touch of rheumatism in the shoulder. My sister makes me sit by the window during breakfast and the draught cuts right across to the door.

MAINWARING   If you're not fit enough for front line action, Godfrey, you shouldn't come at all.

GODFREY   I didn't want to disappoint you.

MAINWARING   Right, stand by to push. Away you go, Jones.

JONES   Dimmer, dimmer, dimmer.

MAINWARING   Jones . . . Jones! This isn't an exercise. It's the real thing. Let in the clutch.

79

JONES   Sorry, Mr Mainwaring, I don't know what I was thinking about.
Jones lets in the clutch.
MAINWARING   Push.
They push. The wheels spin. Pike, behind the rear wheel, gets showered in wet mud.
PIKE   Mr Mainwaring, stop! Mr Mainwaring!
MAINWARING   What are you playing at, Pike? Look at the mess you've made of your uniform.

FRAZER (*holding a bag of sawdust*)   Should we not be using the sawdust, Captain Mainwaring?
MAINWARING   Of course we should. Shove it under the wheel.
Frazer empties the bag.
MAINWARING   Now all push when I give the word. Jones, let out the clutch on my signal.
WILSON   Do you think perhaps Pike should stand back this time?
MAINWARING   Certainly not. If you keep mollycoddling that boy, he'll finish up a complete nancy. Get in your place, Pike. Right, stand by. Push.
He signals to Jones. They all push. Jones lets in the clutch. The wheels spin and eat up the sawdust, which showers over Pike.
MAINWARING   We nearly got it that time.
PIKE   I got it, all right.
Hodges the Warden drives up in his vegetable van. He stops and grins at them.
HODGES (*smugly*)   Hello. Stuck in the mud, are we?
He crosses towards them.
MAINWARING   Ignore him, Wilson. I don't want you to lose your temper with him.
HODGES   Dear, oh dear. Playing at mud pies, are we? You wait till Mummy sees you.
MAINWARING   Right. One more go and we'll be clear.
PIKE   Please can I push somewhere else, Mr Mainwaring?

MAINWARING   Stay where you are, Pike. Stand by, Jones.

FRAZER (*to Hodges*)   Go on laddie—give us a push. Help the war effort.

HODGES   It's no good just pushing it. You've got to lift the back at the same time.

PIKE   Come and lift the back next to me, Mr Hodges.

HODGES   I'm not standing there. All the mud will come flying.

He stands by the cab door. Wilson goes round to Jones at the other side.

WILSON   Jonesey, try reverse and see if we can come out the way we came in.

JONES   That's a good idea. Why didn't I think of that?

He puts the gear into reverse.

MAINWARING   Right. One, two, three—lift.

He signals to Jones. Jones lets in the clutch. The wheels spin in reverse. The Warden is showered with mud.

HODGES   Stop, stop!

MAINWARING   Stop. It's no good.

Jones gets out of the van.

HODGES   You're telling me it isn't. Look what you've done, you ruddy hooligans.

MAINWARING   You'd better try the planks. Get the planks out.

GODFREY   The planks don't seem to be here, sir.

MAINWARING   The planks are not there! Put somebody on a charge, Wilson.

PIKE   Captain Mainwaring, we could take the doors off the van and use those.

MAINWARING   Good idea. Jones, give me a screwdriver.

JONES   You can't do this, Mr Mainwaring. You can't have my doors.

MAINWARING   It won't do them any harm.

JONES   I have no wish to insubordinate, or be mutinous in my manner, Captain Mainwaring, but I have to stand up and boldly defy you, and even threaten you with blackmail.

MAINWARING   What are you saying, Jones?

JONES   I shall cancel your offal, sir, and put your name on my sausage blacklist.

MAINWARING   Now steady on, Jones.

JONES   I have a blacklist, sir, of certain people who I will not supply with sausages, and I shall put your name on the list. I'm sorry, Mr Mainwaring, I never thought I would utter these words to you, but you have driven me to it.

FRAZER   Why don't you ask yon Warden feller to give us a wee bit of a tow?

MAINWARING   Good idea.

WILSON   If I may say so, sir, I think we should be very diplomatic with him.

MAINWARING   Of course I will. (*He shouts loudly as he moves towards the Warden*) Hodges! Come here!

WILSON   That should have done it.

MAINWARING (*to Hodges*)   Be good enough to give us a tow, would you?

HODGES   Me give you a tow? What have you ever done for me?

MAINWARING   There's a large military convoy coming up this road. We are responsible for seeing that it gets to its destination.

HODGES   That's your hard bun, isn't it?

MAINWARING   Very well. In the name of the King I requisition your vegetable van.

HODGES   Oh no you don't. There's a load of logs on that van for the Warden's Post and I'm going to deliver them. If you don't like it, you know what you can do.

He goes towards his van.

PIKE   Why don't you shoot him, Mr Mainwaring?

MAINWARING   Be quiet, Pike.
PIKE   Go on, you've got the authority.
MAINWARING   I said, be quiet Pike.
PIKE   Look, he's trying to drive round. (*He shouts to the Warden*)   You'll get stuck, the same as we did.
The Warden is backing the van onto the field.
HODGES (*from the van*)   Oh no I won't. I won't get stuck because I've got it up here. (*He taps his head*)   I'm going to back round. Then the driving wheels will be leading, like they do in a four-wheel drive. (*He

taps his head again) Here's where you need it, sonny.
He backs the van.
PIKE   You could shoot him, Uncle Arthur.
WILSON   Go away, Frank.
HODGES (*backing the van*)   See, all you have to do is use your loaf.
(*He gets stuck. The wheels spin*) Well, don't just stand there. Give me a push.
WILSON   Do we help him, sir?
MAINWARING   No. Just come away.
They turn and walk away. A bus approaches along the road from the crossroads. It's full of old age pensioners in paper hats. They are escorted by the Vicar. Mainwaring and the group by the van are poised for another push.
FRAZER   Look. Perhaps they'll give us a hand.
The bus halts. The Vicar puts his head out of the window.
VICAR   Are you stuck, Mr Mainwaring?
MAINWARING   Well, only slightly. We'd welcome a few willing hands to give us an extra push, though.
ONE PENSIONER   Come on boys and girls, they need a bit of a push.
The O.A.P.s start to disembark. They are very infirm and are supported by sticks, umbrellas and each other.

MAINWARING   We'll soon be out now.
The frail men and women cross the road and begin to make their way towards the field.
WILSON   I don't think they're going to be very much help, sir.
MAINWARING   Oh, this won't do at all. (*He shouts*) We'll manage, thank you, go back on again.
BUS DRIVER (*shouting*)   Tell you what. I'll just come near enough to tie the rope on, then I'll reverse and pull you out. The ground's all right here. Everybody off. Right, here we go.
GODFREY   Shall I nip up onto the back of the van, sir, and get the tow rope?
MAINWARING   Good idea, Godfrey.
WILSON   Won't he get stuck, sir?
MAINWARING   He's very keen, you know.
WILSON   I mean the bus, sir. Won't the bus get stuck?
MAINWARING   I'm just about fed up with your pessimistic attitude, Wilson. Anyone can see that the ground there is perfectly sound. The driver knows what he's doing.
PIKE   Captain Mainwaring. I thought you ought to know—the bus is stuck.
FRAZER   Captain Mainwaring. I suppose you realise the convoy will be coming down that road fifteen minutes from now?
Mainwaring looks at his watch.
MAINWARING   By Jove, you're right, Frazer.
FRAZER   Lorries will be piled up for a mile or more. Chaos it'll be, sheer chaos. And you'll be responsible. You'll be a laughing stock, a laughing stock. I just thought you ought to know.
WILSON   We could divert them at the crossroads, sir.
JONES   Let me divert them at the crossroads, sir, I should like to volunteer to do that.
MAINWARING   It's five miles away—it would take you an hour, even if you ran.
FRAZER   Which he can't.
PIKE   Look, sir, you could get a lift on that motor cycle.

They see a motor cycle advance, propelled by Yeatman, the Verger, with Mrs Fox in the sidecar.

MRS FOX (*pointing*) Look, it's Captain Mainwaring and lots of people.

VERGER Oh, no! Hide!

MRS FOX I can't hide in this.

VERGER Pretend we haven't noticed them.

The Warden joins them.

HODGES What are you doing with my bike? How dare you?

VERGER It's not your petrol. I pinched it from the Vicar.

Jones arrives.

JONES (*to Mrs Fox*) What are you doing gallivanting with him?

MRS FOX I've got nothing to be ashamed of. Mr Yeatman said he'd take me to pick bluebells.

VICAR Mr Yeatman! I have to warn you that if something has been going on, I may have to reconsider your position in the church.

VERGER Oh, the scandal! The pointing fingers! The wagging tongues! Tittling, tattling, tittling, tattling.

JONES There are no bluebells this month.

MAINWARING Look, you'll have to sort this out some other time. In the name of the King I requisition this motor cycle.

He pushes the Verger off.

HODGES Oh no you don't. I'm going to get a tractor to tow me out.

MAINWARING Then you can drop me at the crossroads.

HODGES All right. Start bumping.

Mainwaring gets on to the back of the bike and Hodges steers the motor cycle towards the field.

MAINWARING What are you talking about?

HODGES Bump up and down to get us through the mud. You've seen them in the scrambles, haven't you?

MAINWARING Pike, get in and bump.

Pike climbs into the sidecar. Hodges endeavours to drive across the mud. Frazer and Godfrey are watching this.

FRAZER Yon Mr Mainwaring shouldn't be doing that at his time of life.

GODFREY In the ordinary course of events we'd all be sitting by the fire, reading something.

HODGES Go on, bump up and down. Bump! Bump!

MAINWARING Pike! Bump!

PIKE I am bumping.

They stick in the mud.

HODGES What's the matter with you? Why don't you keep bumping?

MAINWARING (*breathless*) I am bumping.

FRAZER (*approaching*) We'll manhandle it, sir. (*Mainwaring, Pike and Hodges get off the bike*) Go on—one, two, three, lift!

They lift the bike and take it towards the road. Godfrey is now standing where the bike was.

GODFREY Captain Mainwaring, you've left a little bit behind.

The front and sidecar wheels remain upright in the mud at Godfrey's feet.

HODGES You ruddy hooligans. You've ruined my bike.

JONES You know, Mr Mainwaring, you are very heavy-handed with

vehicles. You should cherish them more and they would respond like-wise.

WILSON   Why don't we use the steam engine to pull us out?

MAINWARING   Because, Wilson, there is no coal.

WILSON   Mr Hodges's van is full of logs.

MAINWARING   I was wondering how long it was going to take you to think of that. Get the wood out of Hodges's van.

HODGES   You're not having my wood and that's final.

PIKE   You really ought to shoot him, Mr Mainwaring.

WILSON   Oh, do be quiet, Frank.

PIKE   We could rub him out, then he wouldn't keep stopping us doing things we want to do.

MAINWARING   Get the wood onto the fire, Frazer.

FRAZER   Aye, aye, sir.

MAINWARING   You know how to drive. Get the roller in position. Pike, disconnect the trailer.

They put some wood on the fire. Frazer blows the whistle and turns the steering wheel. Pike disconnects the trailer. He throws a lever and the organ starts to play.

MAINWARING   Stop that, Pike.

PIKE   I can't stop it, Mr Mainwaring.

OLD PENSIONER   Come on boys and girls. Let's have a bit of a sing-song.

The O.A.P.s, still wearing their paper party hats, start to sing and dance. Pike takes Mainwaring's baton and jams the works. In the process he ruins the baton.

MAINWARING   Stupid boy. Get the steamroller moving.

GODFREY (*to Mainwaring*)   Captain Mainwaring. I've just been thinking. My sister Dolly's Auntie Ethel has a cottage at the cross-roads. I could telephone her from that telephone box. She could divert the convoy. She's only little but she's very determined.

MAINWARING   That might be our best chance of all. Don't you think so, Wilson?

WILSON   It might be our only chance.
MAINWARING   Make the call, Godfrey. Here's two pence.
Jones is giving directions for the moving of the engine towards the phone box.
JONES   Bit more. Bit more—right, that's enough. That's enough. (*The engine rolls on.*) That's enough!
Frazer struggles with the engine, but it moves on. It flattens the phone box as Godfrey approaches with his two pence. The roller passes over the box, leaving the phone between the front and rear rollers. Jones picks up the phone and listens.
JONES   Hello? (*To Mainwaring*) I think the line's out of order, Captain Mainwaring.
Pike points to the wires that are down on the telegraph poles.
PIKE   The wires are down, Mr Mainwaring.
HODGES   You've really done it now, haven't you? That convoy will come piling up on the road and there's nothing you can do about it.
MAINWARING   Don't you believe it. My men will join those together in no time at all. Where there's a will, there's a way.
Later, with Pike sitting on top of the organ trailer and Jones on top of the steamroller, they manage to reconnect the wires.
PIKE   Contact!
JONES   Go ahead, Captain Mainwaring.
Mainwaring, Wilson and Godfrey are kneeling by the phone box.
MAINWARING   Put the two pence in Wilson.
Wilson inserts two pence into the box, which is buried in the ground.
MAINWARING   Over to you, Godfrey.
GODFREY   Ah, good morning. Could you connect me to Walmington-on-Sea 302?

Fade out on a little old lady and a small girl perched on a stepladder in the middle of a deserted crossroads. They are holding a large white table-cloth on which is written 'Convoy Diversion', with an arrow pointing to the right. Both are smiling broadly.

JOHN LAURIE

John Laurie, born in Dumfries, had just completed his architectural studies when the First World War intervened. He joined the Honorary Artillery Company, was wounded at the front, and ended the war as a Sergeant of Musketeers at the Tower of London. Abandoning his earlier plans, he enrolled in a course at Stratford and decided to make acting his career.

Working at the Old Vic and Stratford, he has played every major Shakespearean role, and has appeared in Olivier's films of Henry V, Richard III and Hamlet. Among his other film roles are Johnny Boyle in Hitchcock's Juno and the Paycock and the crofter in The Thirty-Nine Steps. During the Second World War he served in the Home Guard in Paddington.

IAN LAVENDER

Born in Birmingham, Ian Lavender studied at the Bristol Old Vic, then did a season at the Marlowe Theatre, Canterbury, playing juvenile leads. He made his West End debut in 1970 in the musical 'Ann Veronica', and played in Shaw's 'The Apple Cart' at the Mermaid Theatre. In addition to his television work, he has been on national tours with various productions, and played in pantomine for several seasons.

ARNOLD RIDLEY

Born in Bath, Arnold Ridley began acting at the University of Bristol. After serving as a lance-corporal in the First World War, when he was wounded three times, he joined the Birmingham Rep as a resident member and then moved to the Plymouth Rep. In 1923 he wrote 'Ghost Train', the most celebrated of his more than thirty plays.

In the Second World War he gained the rank of major, was posted to France on intelligence work, and later joined the Home Guard in Surrey. His post-war career has included work on radio (nearly twenty years in 'The Archers'), television, and the West End stage.

Privates

Frazer

PRIVATE JAMES FRAZER opened his undertaker's business next door to Jones's butcher's shop in the High Street, soon after he returned form the sea. Born on the Isle of Barra, a wild and lonely place just off the west coast of Scotland, he joined his first ship at the age of fourteen and spent the next thirty-five years roaming the world. Pearl fishing in the South Seas, trading off the coast of Africa, a life packed full of adventure. His stories are legion. How many are true and how many imagined, no one will ever know. He is not an optimist, and his interest in the occult has confirmed his belief that we are all doomed! Doomed!

Pike

PRIVATE FRANK PIKE works in the daytime as a clerk at the bank. He is the youngest member of the platoon, and is very proud of the fact that he carries the Tommy gun. He takes it with him everywhere. When the manager of the local cinema wouldn't let him in because it was a horror film, Pike said that if he was old enough to carry a Tommy gun, he was old enough to see Boris Karloff. He is an avid reader, and takes *Hotspur*, *Wizard*, and *Film Pictorial* every week. His favourite wireless programme is *Happydrome*. He likes it when Enoch says 'Let me tell you.' He says, 'He's even more of a 'Stupid boy' than I am'.

Godfrey

PRIVATE CHARLES GODFREY never did very much at all, except for a period during the First World War when, as a stretcher bearer in France, he won the Military Medal. He never wears it because he feels it would embarrass Captain Mainwaring, who hasn't got any medals. Godfrey worked for forty-five years in the gents' outfitting at the Army and Navy Stores, and returned to live in a small cottage with his two spinster sisters, Dolly and Cissy, at Walmington-on-Sea. As Mainwaring says, he's a useful man to have in a scrap, but unfortunately he's not very good at running about, and he needs to be excused at times. However, he carries the first aid kit, and is nearly always on hand to attend to wasp stings and other hazards of war.

Keep Young and Beautiful

Members of Corporal Jones's section are ambling across a field, carrying a telegraph pole over their shoulders.

MAINWARING   Come on, men, go to it with a will.

JONES   I'm not enjoying this very much.

FRAZER   Yon Mainwaring's taken leave of his senses.

GODFREY   I'm sure it's not very good for the heart.

WALKER   What are you all grumbling about? When the war's over, if anyone wants a telegraph pole delivered in a hurry, we've got ourselves a nice little business.

WILSON   (*observing from a distance*) Don't give up. You really are doing most awfully well.

MAINWARING   Right, gather round. Now this is the sort of thing that's being done by our toughest troops, and if they can do it, then so can we.

PIKE   Captain Mainwaring, could I have something to pad my shoulder?

MAINWARING   No, you can't.

PIKE   But it's red raw.

MAINWARING   There'll be no mollycoddling in my platoon.

WALKER   Trouble is Captain Mainwaring, Jonesey here spent half the time carrying the pole and the other half dangling.

JONES   I was not dangling! Pikey was the one that was dangling.

PIKE   I wasn't dangling—you was dangling!

MAINWARING   All right, that's enough. Now on the command 'Go,' I want to see all three sections charge across the field, go under the tarpaulin and then use their poles to cross the stream. I'll stand a pint of beer to every man in the first section across.

JONES   Right, my section, we're going to win this. I could just do with a pint.

PIKE   Well don't dangle, then.

MAINWARING   Go!

Jones's section moves off before Jones is ready.

JONES   Come on, lads. Charge!

There are three tarpaulins pegged down on the meadow. Sections two and three dive under with their poles and scramble to the other side. Jones's section arrives late.

JONES   Mr Mainwaring! Everything's going round and round.

FRAZER   You old fool—it's you that's going round and round.
WILSON   Come on Jones's section, try to catch up.
Sections two and three have up-ended their poles and let them fall across the stream so that they can use them to shin across to the other side. Jones's section arrives late at the stream, and then up-end their poles.
WALKER   This should be easy for you, Taffy, like tossing the caber.
FRAZER   Belt up or I'll toss you.
They let go of their pole and it falls across the stream.
FRAZER   Come on. You hold it, Pike, and I'll start shinning.
JONES   We're not going to shin, we're walking.
FRAZER   What d'you think this is—a circus?
JONES   Just hold hands and don't look at your feet. Come on. (*He grabs hold of Frazer's hand and leads his section across*) Don't look at your feet, look up—look up—look uuuuuup. . . . *Led by Jones, they all fall into the stream.*

The Church Hall HQ. The platoon, led by Mainwaring, doubles into the hall. The five who fell into the stream are now wearing overcoats.

MAINWARING   Double mark time. (*Exhausted*) Fall out. Officer Wilson.

WILSON   Yes, sir.

As the platoon stagger towards the office, Jones starts to sink slowly to the ground.

FRAZER   (*grabbing him*) He said fall out—not fall down.

JONES   I swallowed so much water my legs won't carry the extra weight.

PIKE   Mr Godfrey, could I come to your place and dry off? If Mum catches me like this she won't let me come any more.

GODFREY   Well we don't have a fire on Wednesdays. Cissy stays in bed with a hot water bottle. You can't get the coal, you see.

WALKER   Don't worry, Pikey. Come back to my place. I'll fit you out with a spare uniform—it won't cost you much.

The side office in the Church Hall. Mainwaring and Wilson enter the office wearily. Wilson sits down heavily.

WILSON   My, my, that was tiring.

MAINWARING   You're out of condition, that's all.

Mainwaring staggers up against the bookcase.

WILSON   Are you all right, sir?

MAINWARING   Yes, of course. Just all that blood pumping through so fast. Makes you a bit dizzy when you stop.

WILSON   I don't think you should have made them double that last two hundred yards.

MAINWARING   Didn't want the ones who fell into the stream to catch cold.

WILSON   (*taking off his boots*) Ah, that's better.

MAINWARING   You won't leave them in here, will you?

WILSON   No, of course not. They did awfully well, didn't they?

MAINWARING   Was a shambles—Jones's section was a joke.

WILSON   They tried very hard though, didn't they?

MAINWARING   That won't be good enough when we're up against Hitler and his Prussian butchers. We shall have to split the platoon into two halves. Those who are young enough and fit enough—and those who aren't up to battle standards.

WILSON   I tried that. It looked rather untidy.

MAINWARING   What do you mean, untidy?

WILSON   Well, there were two in one half and twenty-one in the other.

MAINWARING   I don't mind telling you, Wilson, I sometimes wish I had some younger men under my command.

WILSON   (*picking up a paper*) Others seem to be thinking on the same lines.

MAINWARING   What do you mean?

WILSON   Well, this note has trickled down from the War Office. It recommends that COs look into the age and fitness of their men with a view to getting together with the A.R.P. and exchanging personnel.

MAINWARING   That's an outrageous suggestion—I'll fight that tooth and nail.

WILSON   I do agree.

MAINWARING   I mean . . . how can I face . . . say, Godfrey, or Frazer, or Jones . . . and tell them that I have no more use for them, and they're now in the A.R.P?

WILSON   Well, it seems you won't have to do that. There's going to be a parade and the Area Commander is going to pick out which of us

ought to go to the A.R.P. and which Wardens ought to join us.

MAINWARING · I don't want any of Hodges's rabble in my unit.

WILSON I quite agree, they should leave well enough alone. One just doesn't know where a thing like this would end.

MAINWARING Of course not.

WILSON I mean, take Hodges for instance. You say you don't want any of his rabble in your unit. In fact you might find yourself in the A.R.P. and *this* might finish up as *his* unit.

MAINWARING What on earth are you talking about?

WILSON Well, once they start this sort of thing, I mean, anything can happen.

MAINWARING They wouldn't hand my platoon to a man like Hodges—he's a greengrocer. What does he know about the Army?

WILSON Well, he was in the last lot, you know.

MAINWARING (*rising and going behind Wilson*) That was a different sort of war altogether.

WILSON Still, he did come face to face with the enemy. He looks pretty fit and he's a lot younger than . . . one or two of us.

MAINWARING Meaning me.

WILSON Well, you're by no means decrepid—I mean, you're not exactly Aubrey Smith.

MAINWARING Thank you very much. At the same time, you're not exactly Freddie Bartholomew.

The Church Hall, later the next day. The hall is empty; Mainwaring enters carrying a box under a raincoat. He looks around surreptitiously.

MAINWARING Anybody about? (*There is silence—he moves to the*

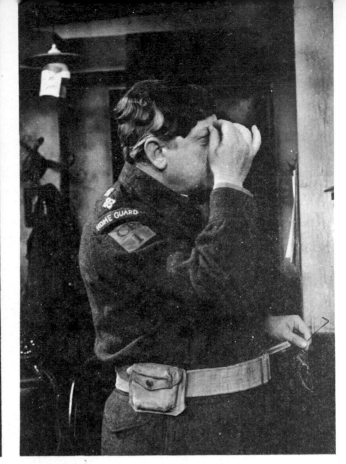

office door and turns. He speaks louder) Is anybody about? (*Satisfied, he moves into the office. He goes behind the desk, ensures that nobody is looking, and then quickly puts the box into a drawer. He hangs up his coat, then goes to the hall door again, opens it puts his head through and calls*) Is anybody there? (*Hearing no reply he closes the door and locks it, then moves stealthily to the outer door and locks that. He stands the black-out frame against the window, then crosses behind the desk. He removes his hat and puts it on the desk, before opening the drawer and taking out the box. He removes something from it, then crosses to the mirror and looks at himself. Rather like a quick change artist he turns away, making a swift adjustment, then turns back to the mirror. He is wearing a toupee, not a very good one, which is gingerish with a small quiff at the front. He contemplates himself critically and makes an adjustment, then tries it without specs.*

He is not quite satisfied, and decides what is wrong. He crosses to the coat stand, takes a box of matches from the pocket of the raincoat, lights one and lets it burn a little, then blows it out. He crosses to the mirror and etches in his eyebrows a little.

Wilson enters the hall, which he crosses, walking very stiffly towards the office. He tries the door.

MAINWARING   Just a moment.

He moves swiftly to the desk, gets the box and is about to put the toupee back but then hesitates and changes his mind. He puts the empty box back in the drawer, picks up his hat and crosses to the mirror. He adjusts his hat.

WILSON   (*calling*) Are you all right, sir?

MAINWARING   Perfectly all right, thank you. (*He crosses to the door and unlocks it*) Sorry to keep you waiting, Wilson.

WILSON (*stopping halfway across the hall*) Oh, I was going round the other way. I thought it was stuck.

MAINWARING No, I was just examining some secret files.

Wilson moves stiffly to the door. Mainwaring notices this but says nothing. He moves behind the desk and sits.

MAINWARING I'm glad you're here early. Sit down. (*Wilson doesn't sit*) I've been giving some thought to our conversation yesterday. Sit down, Wilson.

Wilson makes some attempt to sit, finds it difficult, and straightens up.

MAINWARING I said sit down, Wilson!

WILSON I'd rather stand, thank you, sir.

MAINWARING What's the matter with you?

WILSON I'm rather stiff, that's all.

Mainwaring rises and crosses behind him.

MAINWARING Ah! I see, yesterday's little outing left its mark, did it? Well, I have to confess I have a slight twinge myself this morning—it hits me about there.

Mainwaring puts his hand on the small of Wilson's back. He detects something unfamiliar. Wilson turns quickly as Mainwaring pokes a finger at Wilson's hip.

WILSON Don't do that sir, I'm rather ticklish.

MAINWARING You're wearing corsets! (*Wilson doesn't reply*) Well, am I right?

WILSON Actually, it's a gentleman's abdominal support.

MAINWARING Gentleman's abdominal support, my foot. You're wearing corsets! You're a rum cove, Wilson. You wear that uniform like a sack of porridge, and yet in other respects you're as vain as a peacock.

WILSON It is nothing whatever to do with vanity. I don't want to risk being put into Hodges's mob that's all. I'm really quite proud of our platoon. I think you've done a marvellous job putting us all together. I really mean that. So I think it pays, at the moment, not to look any older than one needs.

MAINWARING I'm sorry, Wilson—it was very kind of you to pay that little tribute. I know that sort of thing isn't easy for a person like you. I was pouring scorn upon you and I had no right to do such a thing. No right at all. I have to tell you that I, too, have taken steps to appear more, well . . . more virile.

WILSON My God, not monkey glands.

MAINWARING Certainly not. Nothing as dramatic as that. What do you think of this?

He removes his hat, revealing the toupee. Wilson collapses, but quickly recovers himself. Mainwaring reacts.

WILSON It is really awfully (*He giggles again*) . . . it's really awfully good.

Wilson subsides into uncontrollable laughter. Mainwaring is furious.

MAINWARING Watch out Wilson, you'll snap your girdle.

The Church Hall. Frazer is in a group with Pike, Walker and Godfrey.

FRAZER Well, the result was—I was beneath him, you follow—now as true as I'm standing here, peeking out from under the brim of his hat was a wee kiss curl.

GODFREY It doesn't sound like Captain Mainwaring at all.

FRAZER Precisely. If you're asking me, he's going funny in the head.

WALKER I reckon one of us ought to go into the office and have a butchers.

FRAZER   I'm not going. I've seen it, I tell you.

WALKER   You go, Pike—you're the youngest.

PIKE   That's not fair, we ought to dip for it.

WALKER   All right, go on then.

PIKE   All right then. Eeney meeney miney moe, catch a nigger by his toe, if he hollers, let him go, eeney meeney miney moe.

Walker gets the moe.

PIKE   It's you.

WALKER   No it isn't. (*He continues the chant*) O-U-T spells out you must go.

Pike is selected.

WALKER   It's you.

FRAZER   Good. Now you'll have to find an excuse to talk to him, and get yourself lower down than he is so you can look under the brim of his cap. You're no' paying attention.

PIKE   He cheated.

WALKER   Never mind about that. Now when you get in the office, you'll have to make some excuse. You tell him you think we ought to go to the local regimental barracks and have more practice at their miniature rifle range.

Jones is talking to Mainwaring and Wilson in the office.

MAINWARING   Well at least we can make everyone as fit as possible, so we'll include one extra period of physical training. You can take that, Wilson.

WILSON   Yes, sir.

JONES   I also think, sir, that as well, and in addition to, also, we should have one hour's instruction in bayonet fighting. We're not doing it as often as we did of yore, and there is no doubt about it, sir, cold steel puts fear into the heart of the Bosch. They do not like it, sir, especially up 'em. I had a very good illustration of this point just outside Wipers. . . .

MAINWARING   Yes, thank you, Jones. I'll make a note of that for next week. You can rejoin your section now.

JONES   Very good, sir.

There is a knock on the door.

MAINWARING   Come in.

Jones salutes, turns about and salutes Pike as he enters. Jones goes.

MAINWARING   (*still standing*) Yes, Pike? What is it?

PIKE   (*saluting*) Excuse me, sir.

MAINWARING   Yes?

PIKE   Barracks.

MAINWARING   I beg your pardon?

PIKE   We haven't done it for a long time, sir.

MAINWARING   What on earth are you talking about, you stupid boy?

PIKE   We ought to shoot at the targets with miniature rifles.

MAINWARING   (*noticing that Pike is behaving strangely in his attempt to see beneath Mainwaring's hat*) Are you all right, Pike?

PIKE   Yes, sir.

MAINWARING   Are you wearing corsets?

PIKE   Am I what?

MAINWARING   I asked you a perfectly straightforward question—are you wearing corsets?

PIKE   I didn't know we were supposed to.

MAINWARING   (*sitting*) Look, start again.

WILSON   I wonder if I could join the platoon? There are one or two things I want to say to them.

MAINWARING   Yes, go ahead. (*Wilson leaves*) Well, Pike?

PIKE   (*kneeling at the desk*) The men asked me to ask you if we could do more of it.

MAINWARING   They surely didn't ask you to pray. Stand up.

PIKE   (*doing so*) Yes, sir. Anyway, we thought, if we could go along to the local one, and borrow theirs, we'd get better at it because we'd have had more practice with the miniature one. (*He deliberately knocks some papers off the desk onto the floor*) Oh dear, how careless of me, I've knocked your papers down, I'll pick 'em up.

Pike dives for the floor, grabs some papers then crawls round the desk to look at Mainwaring. He encounters Mainwaring also kneeling behind the desk ready for him.

MAINWARING   Pike, suppose you tell me what you're up to.

Back in the hall Wilson has the remainder of the platoon gathered round him.
WILSON   The point is this, he's done it because we none of us want to get split up and drafted into the A.R.P.—and let's face it, we wouldn't want to lose him. At the same time, he's very sensitive about it so please try not to stare. Just treat it as a normal everyday thing and for heaven's sake promise me chaps—don't laugh.
Mainwaring bursts in.
MAINWARING   Right, fall in three ranks.
They fall in quickly.
JONES   Fall in three ranks—do as the Captain says, fall in.
They settle.
JONES   We've fallen in three ranks, sir.
MAINWARING   Thank you, Jones. It has come to my notice that a certain aspect of my appearance has given rise to some speculation and a certain amount of hilarity. Now I've never been one for beating about the bush, so here it is straight from the shoulder. I'm wearing a toupee—or a wig, if you want to make it plainer still. If any of you fancy a jolly good laugh at my expense, now's your chance because I'm going to give you a good look at it. Here it is.
He takes off his hat with a flourish. In his haste he catches hold of the toupee at the same time and whips that off inside the hat. We see the normal Mainwaring. The platoon collapse with mirth. Jones and Godfrey at the far end of the line can't see well enough to understand what all the fuss is about.
JONES   (*to Godfrey*) Personally, I think it makes him look older.

Walker is talking on the telephone, surrounded by boxes, sacks and general junk.
WALKER   The point is Mr Hodges, you might find yourself doing left

turns, right turns, under Captain Mainwaring—and you don't get on, do you?

HODGES I'd rather serve under Captain Bligh. (*To an invisible assistant*) Only half a pound of them onions, Beryl. They're like gold. Shove 'em under the counter.

WALKER Now, if your hair was a bit grey like, you wouldn't look quite so young and fit.

HODGES What do you mean young and fit! With my heart and my nerves, I'm a physical wreck.

WALKER Ah, but it's silly to take chances. Now I can let you have something that will whiten your hair instantly. It's pretty expensive, and I can only let you have an ounce—for you it's a quid. Now are you on?

HODGES Well . . . yes. Silly to take any chances, isn't it?

WALKER Good lad—I'll let you have it right away.

He puts the phone down and goes to a tin marked 'ceiling white' where he ladles a spoonful into a small jar.

Outside the door of Frazer's Funeral Parlour at night. Jones and Godfrey approach and knock; the blind on the door is quickly raised to reveal Frazer holding a candle. He opens the door.

FRAZER What's amiss?

JONES We want to talk to you.

FRAZER Come in. Sorry about the candles, but my blinds are too thin for gas-light.

GODFREY I—I like candles. I always think they're much more romantic.

FRAZER Now, what would you be wanting?

JONES Well, it's like this, Jock. Godfrey and I was looking in the mirror, and we decided that if that General was going to pick on anybody to go into the A.R.P. it'll be us three 'cause we're the oldest.

FRAZER You're right—I've not slept at night with dwelling on it.

JONES Remember old Armstrong.

FRAZER Him that passed away last month?

JONES That's the one. Well you made him look not a day over sixty, and he was ninety-seven.

FRAZER Aye it's a skill I ha' with my hands. Ah, it's good of you to say so.

JONES Well—couldn't you do the same for us?

FRAZER Ah . . . I see. It'll be a challenge and no mistake.

GODFREY We'd be very grateful, Frazer.

JONES And we'd see you weren't out of pocket.

FRAZER Ah! Go into the next room and lie on the slab.

The next day in the Church Hall.

WILSON Right, fall in everybody.

PIKE Where's Mr Frazer, Mr Jones and Mr Godfrey, Joe?

WALKER I think they're keeping out of the way till the last minute. When he sees 'em, Mr Mainwaring will have kittens right here.

WILSON Come along, Jones—quick as you can. (*Jones joins platoon*) Get in the ranks, Jones.

JONES Sorry, Sergeant—without my glasses on I'm a bit hard of seeing.

The platoon is drawn up in order for inspection. Right to left, we see Pike, Walker, Jones, Frazer and Godfrey. Jones, Frazer and Godfrey have dark

hair. *Frazer has filled out his cheeks with cotton wool. Godfrey has applied some preparation that has made his skin tight and shiny—the effect is very distinct.*

WILSON   Squad. (*Jones comes to attention*) Wait for it, Jones.

JONES   Sorry, sir. I'm a bit too alert this afternoon.

WILSON   Squad—'Shun.

JONES   Was that better? (*He turns and salutes to Mainwaring*) Platoon ready for inspection, sir.

MAINWARING   Thank you, Jones. Now I think you know me well enough to realise that this inspection by the Area Commander is entirely against my wishes, but orders are orders. Rest assured that if any of you are urged to join the A.R.P. against your wishes, I shall protest to the very highest authority. (*He crosses to Pike*) I think you're safe enough, Pike. (*He moves to Walker*) You too, Walker. (*He moves to Jones, and reacts*) Who the devil's this?

WILSON   Jones, sir.

MAINWARING   Good heavens, what on earth have you done to yourself?

JONES   I didn't want to leave you, Captain Mainwaring, nor these brave troops that you captain and I lance corporal—so Mr Frazer fixed me up.

MAINWARING   Frazer, what's the meaning of this?

FRAZER   (*burbles*)

JONES   He doesn't speak very plainly, sir, on account of cheeks are puffed out with cotton wool.

MAINWARING   Did you know about this, Wilson?

WILSON   Well, I turned a blind eye.

MAINWARING   Well you'd no business to! I'm the only one with the authority to turn a blind eye. (*He turns and sees Godfrey*) Godfrey, what in the name of goodness have you done?

GODFREY   It's one of Mr Frazer's fluids, sir. It tightens the skin.

Mainwaring crosses to Wilson.

MAINWARING   (*to Wilson*). This is ridiculous, he looks like Madame Butterfly. (*To Godfrey*) Get it off at once.

GODFREY   I don't think I can, sir.

MAINWARING   He can't parade like that. How long does it last, Frazer?

Frazer burbles.

JONES   He says he's never dug anyone up to have a look.

Hodges enters in uniform and helmet.

HODGES   Ah, there you are, Napoleon. I just thought I'd let you know that if you've got any ideas about getting me in your shower you can forget it—look.

He takes off his helmet and shows his white hair.

MAINWARING   Very distinguished.

HODGES   Not bad, eh?

WALKER   Wait till he tries to get it off.

MAINWARING   All the same, I don't know why you went to all that trouble.

HODGES   I'd rather look a hundred and seven than serve under you, that's why.

MAINWARING   I see. Pity it doesn't show under your helmet.

HODGES   What? I never thought of that. What the matter—I'll stoop. (*He moves away*) You're not getting me in your squad, Main-

105

waring. The way I'm going on parade they wouldn't have me in the Chelsea Pensioners.

MAINWARING (*to his platoon*) Right, I want you to know that I'm very displeased with this ridiculous charade, but it's too late to do anything about it now, so on your own heads be it.

WILSON I say, that's rather witty.

MAINWARING (*witheringly*) Carry on, Sergeant.

WILSON Yes, sir. Left turn, by the left wheel, quick march.

The Home Guard and the Air Raid Wardens are parading on the barrack square. We see the platoon and about the same number of wardens. The General, followed by the Colonel and Mainwaring, is inspecting the Home Guard. The General does a slight 'take' at the older ones and then passes on. The Colonel salutes and then talks quietly to Mainwaring.

COLONEL He didn't pick any of them—it looks as if you've got away with it.

MAINWARING I sincerely hope so. I really must apologise—

COLONEL (*interrupting*) Congratulations, Mainwaring, you certainly use your initiative in a crisis.

MAINWARING Ah well—we do our best, sir.

COLONEL I didn't see anything, of course. I hope it comes off all right.

MAINWARING I expect it will.

The Barrack Square. Suddenly there is a large flash of lightning.

COLONEL Hello, we're just getting through in time. Give the old man three cheers and I'll buy you one in The Fox.

MAINWARING Yes, sir.

COLONEL Blimey, here it comes.

The rain starts to come down very heavily.

MAINWARING Three cheers for the General—Hip, hip hooray!

As they take off their caps and give three cheers, we cut to Jones, Frazer and Godfrey. Fade out on the dye coursing down their faces.

The Warden,

CHIEF WARDEN WILLIAM HODGES was born in 1897. He started to live the day war broke out. Twice a week all through 1938 he had shut his greengrocer's shop prompt at 5.30 in order to attend A.R.P. lectures on first aid, gas drill, fire fighting, etc. He had put up with the jibes and discomfort, and crawled nose to floor through smoke-filled huts to extinguish practice fires with his stirrup pump or scoop dummy incendiaries into his long-handled shovel. And then on 3 September 1939 he came into his own. He was trained, he was in authority, he could boss people about, tell them what to do. He could order people into shelters when the sirens wailed and blow his whistle when the fire bombs fell.

Within a few months he was wearing the white helmet of the Chief Warden. From then on everyone looked up to and respected William Hodges—everyone except George Mainwaring.

Vicar

THE REV. TIMOTHY FARTHING, Vicar of St Aldhelms, Walmington-on-Sea, is bewildered and unhappy. Who would be a man of God in time of war? How does one propagate the Christian message surrounded by violence and hate? The whole philosophy has to be bent, distorted and half-suppressed in order to fit into a patriotic mould. In his sermons he has to fall back on the usual cliché-ridden drivel. Attendance at Evensong is down to ten and no wonder without an organist. Four of the congregation can't hear and the rest don't listen. The choir, with the exception of that rather nice little fair-haired boy, is rude and unmusical and the Parish Council is unmanageable. Thank heavens that the Vicarage has one cosy room for a study. With a couple of lumps of coal and a cup of hot cocoa life can be almost bearable—and thank heavens for the books.

and Verger

MAURICE YEATMAN, Verger of St Aldhelms—man of iron. That is how he sees himself. Iron discipline, iron will, iron principles and an iron resolve to do what is right and proper for the Vicar. Not that he isn't tempted, mind. A pretty face doesn't stop being a pretty face just because Maurice Yeatman is looking at it. Then there was that Mrs Fox—soft and cuddly, she was—fit to turn the head of a saint. But Yeatman had remembered his position in the Sea Scouts and turned from evil ways and vile pursuits. From time to time the Devil still tries to tempt him. But the iron soul of Maurice Yeatman is not for sale.

BILL PERTWEE

Bill Pertwee had a variety of jobs before becoming an entertainer. He began in show business with a tour of the American bases in Germany, followed by radio work in France and Spain. His first big break came when he was offered a part in 'Ray's A Laugh' on BBC radio; he went on to work for eight years in 'Beyond Our Ken' and 'Round The Horne', and has now made over one thousand radio broadcasts, both as a solo artist and in series. He has also worked in pantomime and summer seasons, and his films include three 'Carry On' productions.

109

FRANK WILLIAMS

Born in London, Frank Williams began his acting career at London's Gateway theatre club. He has since worked primarily on television, including two and a half years as Captain Pocket in Granada's 'The Army Game', and a regular role in Jimmy Tarbuck's ATV show. He has also made several films, appeared in rep and at the Royal Court, and worked in pantomime.

EDWARD SINCLAIR

Edward Sinclair was born of theatrical parents, and made his first stage appearance at six months, carried on in 'The Midnight Mail'. He has spent his life acting, playing almost every kind of role in almost every kind of theatre, from Shakespearean drama to knockabout comedy. More recently, the emphasis has been on films (including 'No Sex, Please, We're British') and television.

THE ARMY THAT NEVER FOUGHT A BATTLE

"At the command 'Fix Bayonets' . . ."

An historical postscript by Norman Longmate

(*Ex-Private 3rd Sussex Battalion, Home Guard. Author of* If Britain Had Fallen; How We Lived Then; *and* The Real Dad's Army.)

Of all the armies ever called upon to defend Great Britain the Home Guard was the strangest: the most traditional and the most novel; the most bloodthirsty and the only one—of its size and firepower—that never actually fought a battle. It was an organisation unique in military annals. Nothing quite like it had ever been seen before and it seems equally certain that nothing quite like it will ever be seen again.

When, on Tuesday 14 May 1940, the government, through the Secretary of State for War, Anthony Eden, called upon able-bodied men aged from seventeen to sixty-five to come forward to protect their localities against invasion it seemed a desperate, unprecedented measure, reflecting the magnitude of the crisis confronting the nation. In fact Mr Eden was doing no more than his predecessors had done for a thousand years, though his appeal was the first to be made by radio, instead of by public proclamation or town crier. The times were too fraught and too busy to indulge in historical reflections, but, had they done so, it would undoubtedly have delighted those first Local Defence Volunteers to realise that by comparison with them even the most ancient Regular regiments were comparative upstarts. No Regular regiment could trace its origins back beyond the seventeenth century. The L.D.V.'s lineage was far longer. Under one name or another, a short-term army of patriotic civilians had been called out whenever danger threatened since Saxon times. Some officials did suggest in 1940 reviving one of these venerable and honourable titles for the new force, like the Volunteers, the Militia or the Fencibles. No one,

SPECIAL ORDER OF THE DAY

BY

COLONEL D. C. CROMBIE, C.B.E.

Commanding No. 2 Battalion (Bideford) Home Guard.

To All Ranks,

This is to convey to you my best wishes for Christmas and the New Year.

We have certain grounds for congratulating ourselves. Half the trying autumn-winter season is behind us. .We have generally managed to keep our tempers, and the Battalion has so far emerged unscathed by Hitler's War of Nerves. And now the shortest day is past. The Black-out Time will gradually get shorter and shorter and the amenities of life will improve from day to day.

But there is no room for self-complacency. It is true that, in pursuing our traditional strategy of striking at the enemy's extremities—where he is weakest—we have gained remarkable successes. But for this very reason we must be on our guard. The enemy is conscious that with every day that passes our military strength increases. He is bound to try to achieve a rapid decision by attacking once more our main citadel—Britain herself.

The enemy must soon become desperate, and a desperate German is more tricky, more brutal, and generally more disgusting, if that is possible, than one who is successfully carrying all before him.

At what time the attack will be launched and whether it will take the form of an air " blitz " alone. or combined with invasion from the sea is uncertain. But come it will.

With the absence of our main striking forces overseas the rôle and responsibilities of the Home Guard are greater than before. I therefore call upon all ranks to fit themselves for the great task which is entrusted to us. In other words—to descend from the sublime to the commonplace—I appeal to you to intensify your training and to make attendances at training parades larger than ever.

It is up to us to hold the fort, to defend this Ancient Castle which for centuries has resisted all assaults of the enemy. The battlements are manned, the portcullis is down, the drawbridge is up, and I give you as your motto for the coming year

" Look to your moat."

(*Sd.*)   D. C. Crombie,
Commanding No. 2 Bn. (Bideford)
Home Guard.

" THERE IS A DEFICIENCY OF CAPS "

however, seems to have favoured the oldest name of all, the fyrd, or, as pronounced, 'the feared'—not, perhaps, a happy title for any army.

But the way in which the Home Guard developed was entirely new, especially in the fantastic, undreamed-of, size of the initial response. Most men in the Second World War waited to be called up to the Forces and answered the summons with reluctance. But recruits queued for hours, pleaded, took years off their true age, almost fought, to be allowed to join the L.D.V. In some places a waiting list had to be opened, as though they were applying for membership of an exclusive club. The government had expected, and wanted, a small force, in rural areas, to look out for parachutists. What it got was a quarter of a million eager volunteers in twenty-four hours, a million and a half in six weeks, drawn from all over the country, cities and hamlets alike, and far from content to act as mere passive observers of an invasion. The L.D.V. was the lightning conductor along which was discharged the country's universal sense of having been pushed about by Hitler long enough and its burning desire to 'have a crack at Jerry'. The boost it gave to morale at home was enormous. 'The response,' reflected Mr Eden, looking back, as Lord Avon, in 1974, 'was a catalyst of the country's spirit and mood at that time.' But the effect abroad was even more important. 'It showed people that we were not pushovers, that there was a mood of resistance in the country which was tough.'

Just as it was the Home Guard, not the government, which decided its own size, so it also carved out its own military role. The government rapidly had to abandon its original conception of a small force of watchers, waiting on village church towers and remote hillsides to Look, Duck and Vanish, as the popular joke had it, if they saw an enemy approaching. The Home Guard's first commanders, mainly retired officers, and early recruits, largely ex-servicemen, despised any such pusillanimous approach. *Their* idea was to engage the enemy at the earliest opportunity, taking pot-shots at his airborne troops as they floated to earth and making him fight thereafter for every road-junction or river crossing. They warmly supported the idea of one staff officer that the country should be defended 'like a bagatelle board, where the ball, falling downwards, hits one pin then another'. Before long, however, as they grew stronger and more confident, most units were unwilling to remain mere 'pins' and sought a more aggressive role. From fighting only small-scale defensive battles, the Home Guard moved on to the creation of fighting patrols which would go out and harass the enemy as he tried to advance, and finally to plans for bringing local units together into powerful task forces which would launch massive counter-attacks in battalion strength, or even more. Instead of leaving each platoon to hide behind hedges or home-made road blocks to ambush or delay the enemy in detail, Zone and Sector Commanders now dreamed of vast encounter battles in the open field

which would make the names of the Avon or the Ouse as famous in military history as those of the Marne or the Somme. The longed-for opportunity never came, though 140,000 Home Guards did see active service of a kind, in Anti-Aircraft batteries, and, for three days just before D Day, the Home Guard in many areas was called out to ward off any attempt by the Germans to interfere with the coming cross-Channel operation. Here, many officers felt, was the vindication of all their efforts and the best answer to their critics: the Home Guard was being called upon to protect the Army.

By this time the Home Guard—the name had replaced that of L.D.V. in July 1940—was better-equipped than any previous part-time army in history; certainly much better than the German *Volksturm*, which made a very poor showing during its reluctant appearance in the closing months of the war. In the summer of 1940 conditions had been very different. Many legends have gathered round those early days and most of them are true. Men *did* go hunting for invading Germans armed only with broom handles and golf clubs. Enterprising commanders *did* raid museums for antique firearms; men *did* stand guard with duelling pistols and even blunderbusses. Patrols *did* go out with one rifle between three men and no more than two rounds of ammunition per rifle. If the advice given to Post Office clerks to hurl pepper at unwanted intruders was never meant to be taken too seriously, the suggestion that dummy land-mines could be constructed of metal soup-plates, to cause enemy tank crews to halt and come out to be ambushed, was actually adopted in some places. The official specifications issued by the Ministry of Supply for two do-it-yourself weapons speak for themselves. The romantically-named *Morning Star* consisted of a mass of barbed wire wound round the end

114

Bank Manager's Adoring Wife : " Oh, Henry ! If only Head Office could see you now ! "

of a broomstick; the graphically-labelled *Flail* could be made by welding a length of doubled-over chain to a gas pipe.

Even less formidable was the first 'weapon' carried by the manager of a Coventry department store, who arrived at the local Drill Hall in 'new suit . . . bowler hat and . . . rolled umbrella. One of the things we had to do was to get down in the prone position, so my rolled umbrella became a rifle'. His next small-arm was only a shade more sophisticated, a wooden rifle, made by the store's carpenter. Another volunteer, then a railwayman in London, armed himself with a stick made from a shunter's pole, which now, in his retirement, forms 'the bottom part of a sea-fishing rod'. The sole anti-tank weapon generally available at this time was the Molotov cocktail, the manufacturing of which did little for the Home Guard's reputation, for frequent calls at the local pubs—to collect 'empties' which could be filled with paraffin and tar—were often misunderstood. In fact beer bottles made poor missiles, being hard to break. Wine bottles were ballistically, as well as socially, superior and the really smart Home Guard also had his own Molotov-carrier, made from sacking or a mattress cover.

One persistent myth, however, ought to be dispelled. The notorious pike was not officially issued in 1940, though some units manufactured spear-like weapons of their own. The first pikes were not distributed from Home Guard stores until 1941 and then much against the wishes of the then Director-General of the Home Guard, Major-General Lord Bridgeman, who was well aware that 'these things . . . might have a poor reception'. Only now can it be revealed why he and his staff failed to defend themselves against the storm of ridicule and disgust which greeted the despised weapon. The instruction to issue pikes

115

" Excuse me, Mr. Benskin, but Mrs. White asked me to tell you that she ain't 'ad 'er bacon ration this week."

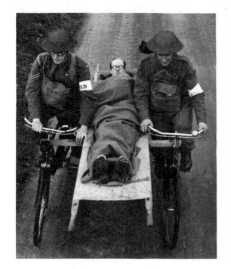

" Hey, you're dead ! "
" No, I'm not. I'm just sort of staggering forward, weak with loss of blood and exhaustion, to recapture our position. . . ."

D. Langdon

came from the Prime Minister himself, his imagination fired by hearing of some of these ancient objects lying unused in the Tower of London, and 'who were we to disobey the orders of Mr Churchill?'

The initial shortage of weapons was due, of course, to the Home Guard's totally unexpected size and to the change in its military role, already described. Instead of having to provide only a few armlets and pairs of binoculars, the War Office found itself besieged by commanders clamouring not merely for uniforms and personal weapons—nearly everyone had both by the end of 1941—but for machine-guns, mortars, anti-tank projectiles and mines, and even artillery. Many of these needs were met by items specially designed for the Home Guard, like the Northover Projector, a drainpipe-like device said to be as dangerous to its crew as to its target if not handled carefully, and the remarkable Smith Gun, which could be towed behind a Baby Austin, but had, most off-puttingly, to be tipped on its side to be fired. On paper, at least, all these weapons added up to an impressive armoury, though how effective some of them would have been in action is doubtful. To say that many Home Guards had no natural aptitude for the military life, much less for handling firearms and explosives, would be an understatement. I once saw a Tommy gun abandoned in a ditch during an exercise by an elderly private who had either forgotten all about it or simply become tired of carrying it around the countryside, while a former member of the BBC Home Guard has not forgotten the day their first hand grenades were issued to his platoon. 'Oh,' remarked the man beside him with interest, eagerly fingering it, 'is this the pin?'

Compared to the Army, the Home Guard had a hard time finding places to train. Many were the platoons forced to have humiliating

arguments with park-keepers about their right to march on the grass, or driven by over-zealous caretakers from school classrooms or church halls where they had set up guard posts. The distinguished retired General commanding a unit in Chelsea found himself burdened with a duty he had never faced in France, having to pacify an irate gardener who expressed 'great indignation . . . when any of our sections rushed some bank to take up a firing position camouflaged among his daffodils'. Later, when the Home Guard was involved in larger-scale exercises, it became notorious for its readiness to bend, or ignore, the rules. In one exercise in Birmingham in 1941, one officer found his position, defending a bridge, overrun by Dutch troops and was given 'a large number of casualty labels' by the umpire and told to distribute them. 'With great presence of mind,' recalled his admiring commander, 'he handed them all out to the Dutchmen,' who, knowing little English, politely accepted them. Another unit, at Colwyn Bay, becoming weary in the small hours of Sunday during an all-night exercise, 'decided to be . . . typical Huns and to attack a first aid post, which looked hospitable . . . Soon stretchers were laid down, blankets provided and our commando in repose.'

Such incidents perhaps revealed that mysterious quality often referred to, the 'Home Guard spirit'. Lord Bridgeman concluded that 'the Home Guard spirit to a large extent, though not entirely, meant that people would rather do what they wanted instead of what they were told'. There was, however, an atmosphere about the Home Guard totally different from that of the Army, as everyone who served in both, as I did, will probably agree. Until February 1942, when conscription was introduced to keep units up to strength and existing members were given the option of resigning or remaining in till the end of the war, every man taking part in a Home Guard parade was there because he wished to be. If he tired of being a soldier he had only to give a fortnight's notice, under the famous 'housemaid's clause', and he could hand in his rifle and uniform and go home. Very few ever did, but had a similar rule existed in the Regular forces most barrack rooms would soon have been remarkably empty.

Apart from consisting at first solely of volunteers, the Home Guard also escaped that rank-consciousness so universal in the Army. Until November 1940 there were not even any ranks and salutes and 'sirs' were given by choice or not at all. Even after the coming of commissions and N.C.O.s relations between all the members of a unit remained, by Army standards, remarkably free and easy. 'Officers Only' signs were rarely seen on Home Guard premises and, in spite of grumbling from some ex-Regular officers, all ranks travelled third-class on the railways and received the same allowances for the use of a car or bicycle on duty. The Forces were depressingly full of N.C.O.s bawling threats of 'charges' and 'the glasshouse'. In the Home Guard persuasion was more common than prosecution; the watchword most valued was comradeship, not discipline. Most important of all, perhaps, since the local inn became for many units a second headquarters, was that a Regular officer was expected to leave a bar when an Other Rank entered it; the pub, by contrast, was where Home Guard officers got to know their men best.

How this unique, democratic, essentially amateur force, so different in every way from the fiercely professional German army, would have fared in action one can only speculate. My own belief—and I saw the Home Guard from inside as that most typical of members, a private in a General Service, or ordinary infantry, Battalion (though only late on in its history, in 1943)—is that it would not have lasted very long. Even Regular units need to be 'blooded' by experience in action, but by the time we had learned the lessons needed for survival, the battle would have moved on. Paradoxically, the Home Guard would probably have been most valuable at the very beginning, in 1940, when it was asked to do a job well within its powers, to watch and warn. The military historian Basil Collier (author of the volume on *The Defence of the United Kingdom* in the official war history series) agrees. 'The Home Guard,' he believes, 'would have done a good job as a body of watchers and scouts, but I can't see them playing a major role in repelling any kind of invasion. Indeed I would think that commanders of regular troops would have wanted to keep the Home Guard out of the way so as to keep the roads clear for their own troops and supplies.'

The Home Guard's birth had been dramatic; its end was sad. Late in October 1944 the government suddenly announced that the whole force would be stood down in only three days' time. Dismissed as no longer wanted, the 1,700,000 men then in the organisation received no gratuities, no medals, no civilian suit, though, after an argument, they were allowed to keep their battledress and their boots. But the nation did say 'Thank you'. On Sunday, 3 December 1944 there were official farewell parades all over the country. In most places the rain poured down and the wind howled; the dripping soldiers, anxious to get under shelter, could not even hear the speeches praising their efforts. One man from a rocket battery, who took part in the big parade in Hyde Park, vividly remembers what happened as his column neared the saluting base and received the order 'Eyes left!': 'My tin hat fell clean down over my ears and I didn't dare adjust it . . . I didn't even see the King.' At Colwyn Bay in North Wales, one member of the 11th Denbighshire Battalion remembers how 'Colonel Llewellin loomed through the driving mist and sleet' and 'gave the order, for the last time, "Home Guards and Auxiliaries dismiss!"' Symbolically, the regular rigid lines broke and dissolved into a horde of individuals seeking shelter from the storm . . . The show was over. It was still raining.' It was also a very British ending to a very British enterprise.

In the years when our Country was in mortal danger

J. H. Gaston

who served 9th June 40 to 31st Dec '44 gave generously of his time and powers to make himself ready for her defence by force of arms and with his life if need be.

George R.I.

THE HOME GUARD

RECTOR TO SUE H.G.

ALTHOUGH War Office officials have apologised to the Rector of Newchurch, near Leigh, Lancs, following his arrest by the Home Guard last month, it is not intended to let the matter rest there.

The announcement yesterday by the Archdeacon of Warrington stated that legal proceedings were being taken on behalf of the rector —the Rev. H. E. Elrington Reed, because "the reputation of a man of splendid character is at stake."

Mr. Reed complained at the time that he was detained by the Home Guard and held for questioning by their commander, Mr. F. Crampton, a Leigh solicitor.

Resigned

The incident occurred when two members of the Home Guard took the rector to their local headquarters after he had refused to hand over the key of an empty school. After about fifteen minutes the rector was allowed to return to his home.

The matter has caused such feeling that Mr. Crampton resigned his command, only for eighty men of the Home Guard to hand in their own resignations in sympathy.

Yesterday, however, it was stated that following a personal appeal from Mr. Crampton, the men would carry on.

Both Mr. Reed and Mr. Crampton decline to discuss the matter, but the Archdeacon of Warrington said yesterday: "The War Office has inquired carefully into the matter and has apologised amply to Mr. Reed."

HOME GUARD TURNS BACK FIRE BRIGADE

They Had No Identity Cards

From " Daily Herald " Correspondent
CARDIFF, Monday.

MR. WALTER DAVIES, chief of the fire brigade at Tredegar, Monmouthshire, has handed in his resignation.

This, he told me to-night, is why:—

"When an air raid alarm was sounded in the district, members of my brigade, all volunteers, rushed into their uniforms.

"They were making their way on foot to the fire station when the Home Guard held them up.

"The firemen were asked to produce identity cards. These had been overlooked in the men's hurry to don their uniforms, so the Home Guard turned them back.

"This caused a delay of three-quarters of an hour before the fire engine could be manned. The consequences might have been serious.

"I should have thought the uniform would have been good enough to pass my men through. Most of them were actually known to the Home Guards. I don't ask my wife to produce her identity card!

"As a protest against this indignity to the fire brigade uniform I have handed in my resignation.

HOME GUARD PATROLS
WITH BOW AND ARROW

Daily Express Staff Reporter

WHEN Mr. John Davey, of Thornton Curtis, near Grimsby, goes on patrol as a Home Guard platoon commander, he carries a revolver and bow and arrows.

He is archery champion of the north of England, and he holds that a bow would be an effective weapon in some circumstances even in modern war.

"Think," he said to me yesterday, "of the effect on a group of Germans if one of them suddenly dropped with an arrow through him.

"They would have no idea where the arrow came from. They would be terrified."

Mr. Davey estimates that an arrow would "get its man" at 200 yards, although for practical purposes a shorter range would be necessary.

"I should be pretty sure of a hit at fifty or sixty yards," he said. "At thirty-five yards an arrow would be deadly."

Ready for a " S

We can rely on the Home Guard ! grand old soldiers in this voluntary only increased by the enemy's threa purposeful men deserve the best of H.P. Sauce, which they add with r meals they snatch betwe